"When people think of revelation, they often mistakenly think only of judgment and the destruction of the world. This book, *A Resurrected Cosmos*, captures the true essence, the new world, and reality God is preparing for his people. I recommend strongly not just reading but meditating on the themes uncovered in this excellent work. In actuality, we are citizens of heaven/the New Creation, and this will help us realize our wondrous present as well as our glorious future. Our lives will be changed, and we will see everything a lot more clearly as a result. It is exciting to see this extremely positive work on the Apocalypse come to light."

—Grant R. Osborne, author of *Revelation: Verse by Verse* and *The Hermeneutical Spiral*

"In this extremely well written piece, Brayden Brookshier effectively identifies common misunderstandings concerning redemptive history, while directing the reader to a more biblically precise way of discussing the major themes of Revelation. Brookshier's use of both creative illustrations and scholarly analysis makes *A Resurrected Cosmos* an absolute must-read for anyone seeking greater clarity regarding the eternal hope promised to those in Christ Jesus."

—J. D. Eldridge, President, Branch College

"I've been reading and studying Apocalyptic literature all my life. It has been decades since I've read a book on Revelation that captured my imagination. Brayden Brookshier in his book *A Resurrected Cosmos* not only challenged my thinking but presented some fresh ideas that pushed me out of my proverbial box and beyond! I loved his take on 'heavenizing earth.'

Frankly, the majority of scholarly works I've read on Revelation leave me feeling guilty. Guilty for yearning for some version of heaven that feels a little like my home, planet earth. Brayden applied scholarly exegesis to Revelation and the results are exciting. I hope you will take the time to read *A Resurrected Cosmos*. I promise you won't feel guilty but rather exhilarated about heaven, earth, and a glorious future!"

—Steve Bombaci, Pastor, Newbreak Church Pacific Beach

"Ever find yourself a bit fearful of the Book of Revelation—or a bit too nonchalant about what it actually means for your life? Then let me introduce you to Brayden Brookshier, who unveils a treasure trove of truths about the final book of the Bible. These aren't just nuggets, folks. These insights are the kind that should have followers of Christ everywhere both lifting our hands in awesome wonder and bowing in the [face] of such beautiful hope. After reading this book, I'm convinced you'll see

Revelation in an entirely new light and start to think of the last book of the Bible as the bridge to a new book—a living book in which you're one of the characters—that's far better than you've ever dared to imagine."
—Caleb Breakey, author of *Sermon Crunch: Write a Powerful Sermon in Half the Time*

A Resurrected Cosmos: The Drama of Revelation as the Unveiling of New Creation

A Resurrected Cosmos: The Drama of Revelation as the Unveiling of New Creation

Brayden Rockne Brookshier

Fontes

A Resurrected Cosmos: The Drama of Revelation as the Unveiling of New Creation

Copyright © 2023 by Brayden Rockne Brookshier

ISBN-13: 978-1-948048-91-0 (paperback)

All rights reserved. No part of this publication may be reproduced, stored in a retrieval system, or transmitted in any form or by any means—electronic, mechanical, photocopy, recording, or any other—except for brief quotations in printed reviews, without the prior permission of the publisher.

Scripture quotations, unless marked otherwise, are from the Lexham English Bible. Copyright 2012 Logos Bible Software. Lexham is a registered trademark of Logos Bible Software.

Typeset by Monolateral™ in Minion 3 and Museo Sans.

FONTES PRESS
DALLAS, TX
www.fontespress.com

Contents

Acknowledgements xvii

Preface xv

Introduction: The Most Extraordinary Letter 1
   The Apocalypse: It is Not the End of the World 2
   Why This Book is Needed 3
   Our True Eternal Hope 4
   Five Key Movements 5
   A Note on the Genre of Revelation 6
   Key Terms Defined 8
   Conclusion 11

1. Less Like a Home, More Like a Train 13
   Why Did God Create Everything? 13
   God is Love Because God is Triune 15
   Was Eden "Perfect"? 17
   A Garden that Needed Guarding 18
   The First Sin 20
   A Place of Probation and Potential 23
   Preconsummate Stage 24
   The Promised Eternal State 26

2. The Emerald Throne 31
   Behind the Scenes 32
   World of Color 33
   The Throne Room 36
   The Song Without Cease 39
   Casting Crowns 42
   Equal Rewards 44
   Only God Is Worthy 49
   Sing to Yahweh a New Song 50
   Excursus: Eternal Life 51

3. The Scroll of Salvation 55
   Who Is Worthy? 56
   Behold the Lamb 58

  A Final Sacrifice 62
  God Will Set All Things Right 65

4. THE CORONATION OF HEAVEN'S KING 69
  The Royalty of Jesus 70
  The Coronation 72
  Jesus the Prince 75
  A New Song 76
  The One Who Is Worthy 77
  The Multicultural People of God 80
  Ear-Shattering Worship 82
  God and the Lamb 83
  The Wrath of the Lamb 84
  Paving the Way for the Parousia 86

5. THE WEDDING OF TWO WORLDS 89
  A Kainos Creation 90
  A Sea-less Existence 92
  Recreation in the New Creation? 97
  Heaven on Earth 99
  The Death of Death 103
  God with Man 106

6. GOD'S THESIS STATEMENT 109
  The Thesis of Redemption 109
  My Imagination Ceased 112
  Who Is the Alpha and the Omega? 114
  What is Excluded from the New Creation? 116
  What About Hell? 117
  The Father's Love for Us 120
  The Eschatological Nature of Resurrection Bodies 123

7. THE MOST HOLY PLACE 129
  The New Jerusalem: A People and a Place 130
  God's Global Temple 134
  No Need for a Temple 137
  City of Light 140
  Infinitely Happy in an Infinitely Happy God ... 143
  Eden in Our Hearts 147

8. THE WORLD CREATED FOR THE SON 149
    Paradoxically Nostalgic and New 150
    The Life-Giving Garden 150
    The Tree of Life 153
    Looking into the Eyes of the Creator.................... 157
    The Kingdom of the Son................................. 164
    Jesus Is So Much More 167

9. CONCLUSION: THE END IS THE NEW BEGINNING 169
    Welcome to Chapter One................................. 170
    Where Do We Go From Here?........................... 172

BIBLIOGRAPHY 175

Acknowledgements

To my wife, Ariana: You have continually supported me and inspire me to study, write, speak, and lead. You deserve a lot of credit for all that I do.

To my son, Kairo: I pray this vision of new creation captures your imagination and bolsters your allegiance to King Jesus.

To the many small group settings over the years where ideas in this book where worked out (special shoutout to a few attenders from Newbreak Church: Bruce and Jodi Kliewer, Andrea Richardson, Rhonda Petrosky, Heather Britt, just to name a few): Our conversations have re-enforced the need for a book like this. Please know I always felt our conversations were mutually beneficial.

And a special thanks to Cliff and Todd with Fontes Press. You guys believed in this manuscript. Thanks for bringing it to fruition in new light!

Preface

Choosing a title for this book was challenging, second only to the hard work of trying to summarize the goal of this book (see the Introduction)! But this book is a labor of love as I worked through a vision of the Christian hope, especially through the lens of the often-feared book of Revelation. The unedited version of this book was first finished in 2017. To put that in perspective, the year is 2023 now. And while the book did exist in a self-published format (previously: The Dawn of the New Creation), it lacked the authenticating stamp of a publisher. I believed the ideas in this book were too important to be kept in the world of self-publishing. In 2020 Fontes Press expressed interest in it, and the rest is what lies ahead in this book.

Why do I give this brief backstory? One reason is because the foremost endorser—New Testament scholar, Grant Osborne—passed on to be with the Lord from the time he endorsed the self-published version until now. I believe it is important to express that the manuscript he endorsed is still in tact. Fontes Press has given this book further credibility and enhanced the reader's experience from an editorial perspective. However, over the span of the 7 years from its original composition and review from endorsers, the book's integral message and the heart of the arguments have been maintained. Having had a variety of opportunities to teach on this material from 2017 until now, I can say with confidence that I have doubled-down on everything written here. Thus, I feel especially excited to release this book, seven years in the making, technically, as I believe the ideas expressed here have been worked through a wide range of Christians spanning across a few denominations. I know eschatology can be a polarizing topic, and where I have an interpretation that might not suite your own, I ask for your captive attention. Hear me out, as I would you.

At the end of the day, I have been deeply encouraged by how much we (the various expressions of Christian thought represented through denominations) are still orthodox in our Christian beliefs and practices. Our eschatology might have some diversity, but let us not divide so easily on these things. Hence, I decided there were a few topics not even to make a comment on in this book, not because I don't find them mildly important or interesting (on the contrary!) but because this book is meant to be keenly focused on the eschatological vision we can trust, even though we cannot see all the details of how it will fall into place. Yes, there will be some mystery, and you'll get to read parts where I have to speculate, but those will be limited (I promise!). More than anything, I hope reading this book excites you. We are talking about a vision of *A Resurrected Cosmos* after all! I pray this draws you closer to the heart of your Savior. And I thank you for taking the time to come alongside me on this journey. It'll be thought-provoking and engaging. I say this because here I am, seven years after writing this manuscript, and I could not be more excited to continue to dwell on these passages of Scripture and the message they contain.

- Brayden Rockne Brookshier, May 2023

Introduction

The Most Extraordinary Letter

> "And the seventh angel blew the trumpet, and there was a loud voice in heaven saying, "The kingdom of the world has become the kingdom of our Lord and of his Christ, and he will reign forever and ever."
>
> —Rev 11:15

Revelation is the most extraordinary book of the Bible—both literally and literarily! This circular letter is written in a genre completely foreign to the modern world. We simply do not have modern writings quite like apocalyptic prophecy. We have various genres of fiction and various genres of non-fiction. Apocalyptic literature, however, is unique in that its description of reality (whether that of the present or the future) is characterized by its use of metaphor and symbolism. It stimulates the imagination as much as it informs the reader of its message.

Revelation is the final book of the biblical canon and was written by the last living apostle—John. It was likely written during the last decade of the first century while John was living in exile on the island of Patmos, separated from the churches he once ministered to. There, John received a vision from the resurrected Jesus, one that would encapsulate a fitting letter to encourage the Christians of Asia Minor who were facing tumultuous times because of their faith in the risen Christ.

The letter of Revelation is especially concerned with the topic of eschatology, which is the study of last or final things. Because Revelation addresses the end of human history as we know it and the beginning of the new world, it is appropriate for Revelation to be the last book of the Bible. This brings us to the purpose of this book.

The Apocalypse: It is Not the End of the World

The reason for this book is to demystify the Christian's ultimate hope. Instead of the more popular notion that heaven is the ultimate hope for the believer in Christ, I will argue this hope is encapsulated by the phrase *new creation*. My desire is to illustrate how John's message of Revelation was not intended to cause confusion. Yet, when we read Revelation in light of the whole biblical drama, we find that its central message is actually quite clear and comprehensible. After all, the well-known title of the letter, "Revelation," was not meant to conceal truth but to unravel it before you with vivid imagery.

Revelation opens with the "apocalypse" of Jesus Christ. Apocalypse, in the original Greek, literally means "revelation." It is an unveiling of something previously not known. What exactly is being revealed? Jesus Christ is, but also "what must soon take place" is being declared (Rev 1:1). Again, the purpose of Revelation is the opposite of hiding the truth from us. Instead, it is a recapitulated unveiling of truth.

At the time Revelation was written, Jewish expectation anticipated God making all things right and establishing a new world under the Messiah's rule. Part of the expectation meant a reversal of the wrongs that have plagued humanity since its fall in the Garden. Through Jesus the world will be transformed in such a way that can only be described as new creation. This was the ultimate hope of the Messiah's Jubilee (cf. Isa 61). The major plot of Revelation is the unveiling plan of God's kingdom coming to transform all of creation. It reveals how God is bringing redemptive history to its consummate state of glory because of the victorious work of Christ—who has become the King of heaven and earth—and will one day bring His kingdom reality to the entire cosmos. The drama is dire and requires intense language to convey how in the end

God wins. The goal of God bringing about his new creation will be realized, despite any and all resistance towards it.

However, please do not settle for this overly brief explanation. The rest of this book is an "unveiling, " if you will, of the primary plot in Revelation—and the Bible—coming to a head with the ultimate hope all Christians can agree upon—new creation.

Why This Book is Needed

I heard countless sermons growing up about heaven—I am sure many share my experience. Between the church camps, altar calls, and small groups, heaven was a lighthearted topic of hope and joy. As I began to read the Bible and grow in my knowledge of God's Word, however, I began to notice something different. What I began to perceive is that the more common, westernized concept of heaven did not fully line up with what the Bible taught.

The idea that when we die our highest hope is to fly away to heaven—which is what I had always heard—was not making sense, biblically. It is not that a different gospel was being preached, but rather a misunderstanding of our eternal hope. I became passionate about this topic and vigorously studied it to see what the Bible truly had to say about heaven. The desire to know God's Word and what it says about our great salvation is the very inspiration behind the writing of this book.

The concept of new creation is a dominant theme in the biblical narrative. This single eschatological ("end goal") lens can unlock numerous avenues for understanding the intention of the redemptive drama.

More specifically, Revelation is a deep book, so I am going to take the approach of homing in on the lens of new creation, so that we can see how two major key movements of the book reveal this ultimate biblical goal, which has been anticipated from the opening verses of Genesis.

In light of this, the entire Bible is eschatological, it keeps the *end goal* in mind from the beginning. The narrative arc encompasses the cumulative journey toward new creation as the purpose and goal of the biblical plotline. It can even be said that new creation has been central to the ancient Jewish hope all along.[1]

Before we begin exploring the riches of the book of Revelation it will be helpful for me to lay out clearly what my thesis is: *The climax of the story of redemption is a resurrected cosmos where the triune God and His redeemed, resurrected people will reign for eternity, unrivaled and infinitely satisfied with endless chapters of adventures to experience.*

Therefore, for the believer in Christ, heaven is only the penultimate hope. Even heaven points toward the restoration of all things and subsequent new creation that the ultimate hope of the believer is found.

Our True Eternal Hope

Interestingly, in Revelation the word for heaven, *ouranos*, is never used to describe the final state of believers. It is used either to describe the dwelling place of God or of the physical starry expanse. Technically, *there is not a single verse in the Bible* that speaks of believers going to heaven when they die. This should be shocking considering how many of our gospel presentations include such phraseology. I want to propose we return to more biblically accurate language to talk about our eternal hope. In fact, you would be hard pressed to find a single verse in the New Testament that uses the terminology of heaven in conjunction with either where we go when we die or our ultimate hope. Why is that? This is because heaven is not the end of the story for the believer.

As Christians, how can we tell others about our glorious salvation if we do not even know what the Bible says about the destiny of creation? In this book, I hope to give you a chance to fall in love again with eschatology.

Many Christians reserve the study of eschatology for the academically trained or spiritually elite. I suggest that the lens of new creation not only unlocks ancient treasures in the Bible, but also helps our hearts live more profoundly in the present, alive to the

---

[1] Donald Macleod, *Jesus Is Lord: Christology Yesterday and Today* (UK: Christian Focus Publications, 2000), 150.

wonder of God's redemptive work, which has begun in the present but will culminate in the future.

My hope for this book is that it would provide you with a biblical foundation for the utmost confidence and celebration of your eternal hope as a Christian. Hope, when grounded in Scripture, is not an existential wish that may or may not happen. Instead, hope that is rooted in the Bible gives us an unwavering confidence, and such a hope is something humanity desperately longs for. In fact, hope is the very oxygen that prolongs our endurance.

This book is all about how the new creation, specifically as it is described in Revelation, gives us a hope that fills our hearts with bounding joy that compels us to give our lives to share this hope with everyone that we possibly can. In this way, my aim is to focus on the aspects of eschatology that are most pertinent and clear, without having to divulge into plenteous speculation. We will be utilizing Revelation as the primary text, while at times detouring elsewhere to show an integrated view of these things in all of Scripture.

Five Key Movements

In my studies of Revelation, I have discovered five explicit and preeminent key movements that will culminate in new creation: exhortation to the churches (chapters 1-3), the throne room vision (chapters 4-5), apocalyptic judgment (chapters 6-18), eschatological salvation (chapters 19-20), and the new creation (chapters 21-22).[2]

All of these point toward the unveiling of the exalted Christ and His sovereignty over human history. Thus, Revelation is supremely theological and theocentric, highlighting the triune God as the center of all things. Our focus will be in exploring and exegetically walking through two key movements: the throne room vision (Rev 4-5) and the new creation (Rev 21-22). While every verse in Revelation is important to the overall understanding of the book,

---

2 Admittedly, these are oversimplified and are not meant to be an exegetical outline of the book. Think about this more as a 30,000-foot overview of the structure.

some inevitably get lost in the details and interpretive difficulties present in Rev 6–20. Somewhere along the way questions about the meaning of the seals, trumpets, or the millennium seem to supersede what Revelation is climaxing toward—the promise of new creation (Rev 21:1–22:5).

Because the goal of this study is not to explain everything in Revelation, but to put the emphasis where Revelation wants it to be, I encourage you to use other resources to study the issues and passages not addressed in this book. I promise, the journey will be worth it if you will allow me to be your guide through this challenging, yet exhilarating, letter.

For that very reason, I will be offering very few comments on Rev 6–20. The reason for this is twofold. First, we can understand the message of Revelation sufficiently by focusing on the two particular events recorded in Rev 4–5 and 21–22. And second, I approach Rev 6–20 with extreme humility. I try to be honest with those whom I teach. When I have a confident tone about a particular text or idea, I want it to mean something. On the other hand, I have no trouble admitting that I am unsure about something. And again, whether my speculations about some of the details of Rev 6–20 are right or wrong, it is superfluous to the main thrust of what I will communicate in this book.

So, we will not be investing ink and pages discussing the antichrist or millennial views—though, I have no problem laying my cards out to show what I think regarding those questions. Yet, whether I am right or wrong about the millennium, for example, the main point of this book—pointing to the ultimate, future hope of new creation—is something I am much more certain of and is compatible with diverse views of what can or will happen prior to then.

A Note on the Genre of Revelation

If you have ever tried reading Revelation you may have noticed that it is odd, or perhaps even befuddling! Perhaps more than any other New Testament book, the book of Revelation requires the guide of an aide to assist in your reading. I hope to be that for you as you move through the pages of this book, at least in the passages, topics, and themes that we will discuss.[3]

The first issue we need to address is the symbolic language embedded in the message of Revelation. Grant Osborne highlights an important note on apocalyptic symbolism: "Those who take it as completely literal miss the very nature of the apocalyptic genre, yet to take it as entirely symbolic misses the mark as well. In Jewish apocalyptic literature, the two aspects are blended and interdependent, and each symbol must guide us as it functions in its context."[4]

That presents us with a challenge when interpreting the book of Revelation. We cannot over-spiritualize it, making everything symbolic; however, we cannot read apocalyptic literature in the same manner as we would read the newspaper, either. We must read Revelation as an apocalyptic prophecy functioning as a letter of exhortation to real churches in the latter part of the first century. How literally or how symbolically we read Revelation is the inherent challenge every interpreter faces when they come to the final book of the biblical canon.

Ultimately, the symbolism communicates a coherent message—one of hope. Revelation is not a roadmap about the end of the world. Revelation is not a puzzle that requires decoding. Although John uses vivid symbolism, the symbols that he utilizes can be interpreted both by a familiarity of the ancient world as well as through a comparative study of similar apocalyptic texts that predate the book of Revelation.

The task for the modern-day reader is to examine Revelation through ancient eyes. Everything introduced here, while having modern relevance, is rooted in a careful examination of the historical context and grammatical analysis of the text of Revelation.

---

3 For those things I do not address I would point you to the bibliography at the end of this book. Any resource listed there does not necessarily mean I agree with all the author's conclusions. However, I think it is good for Christians to read those who they agree with in full and in part, even more those who they disagree with. So, for those who want to know more than what is stated in this book I would encourage you to consult the bibliography.

4 Grant R. Osborne, *Revelation: Verse by Verse*, Osborne New Testament Commentaries (Bellingham: Lexham Press, 2016), 374.

Key Terms Defined

Before moving on, it will prove helpful to provide definitions for several important terms that will be addressed in this study. This will ensure that we are on the same page as we continue through the following chapters.

The fall—the defining moment in Gen 3 is Adam and Eve's rebellion against God. Their choice to rebel introduced not only sin, but all the physical and spiritual consequences of sin into the world.

Trinity/Triune—the word that encapsulates God's nature being three distinct persons (Father, Son, and Holy Spirit) but one eternal deity. Because Scripture usually speaks of "God" as specifically God the Father, it is helpful to use the terminology found in Ephesians 4, namely that is there is one God (the Father), one Lord (Jesus Christ), and one Spirit (the Holy Spirit), which are distinct in person but one in essence.[5]

Salvation—God's rescue or deliverance of His people. In the Old Testament, the Exodus was the dominant salvific event; in the New Testament, it is the cross. By trusting in Jesus, humanity is rescued from sin's penalty and power and saved for God's glory. Upon trusting in the Lord Jesus, individuals receive the Holy Spirit as a gift to guide them and transform their lives. Salvation is far more than holistic than the soul's moral restoration or anything of that sort. Salvation is about the whole human being redeemed and transformed, body and soul, along with the entirety of creation. While certain passages may highlight a certain aspect of salvation, the concept is far broader and richer.

Eschatology—that which is concerned with the study of last or final things. It is not always limited to the talk of chronological "last" things, but it can also refer to the ultimate fulfillment of the intended purpose of something. This can be used as an adjective, "eschatological," to dress up a certain word, describing the end goal

---

[5] For lay-level discussion on the Trinity listen to Adventures in Theology (podcast) episode number 45 [http://tiny.cc/AdventuresInTheology]. In this episode I converse with Abdu Murray (of RZIM) on understanding and delighting in the Trinity.

with a sense of ultimacy. For example, Jesus is the "Greater Davidic King," which is an eschatological, typological fulfillment, but it is in the past in regard to our timetable. That is why the topic of eschatology needs to be parsed into what is inaugurated and what is future-oriented (see below).

Inaugurated Eschatology—that which began and is true now. While it may be awaiting a greater fulfillment, much of Christian eschatology has an "already/not yet" paradoxical tension. God's redemptive work is initiated but has not culminated. Synonyms include initiated, commenced, and launched. The kingdom of God/heaven is a perfect example of this. It has been inaugurated ("already"), but the greater realization of it still lies ahead for when Jesus returns to finish what he began ("not yet").

Future Eschatology—that which will be fulfilled in the future; something that has not happened yet. For example, the ushering in of the new heavens and new earth simply has not taken place yet; that is anticipated in the future. Typically, in biblical eschatology it is important to maintain that the confidence of certainty of something coming to fruition is grounded in God's promise to make it so.

Eschaton—Greek for "end" or "last," referring to the return of Christ and the end of history. It is a word pregnant with meaning, alluding to the end and ultimate culmination of God's sovereign plan. This includes the return of Christ and the final judgment when God will eradicate the world of sin and its effects and usher in the new heavens and the new earth. Eschaton is shorthand for the return of Jesus (also known as the "second coming" or the "*parousia*").

Heaven—in biblical literature, heaven can simply mean the starry expanse visible above us. It can also mean God's abode in a dimension different from our own. Believers who have died and are with the Lord right now are in heaven in the sense that they are in God's abode and presence. In modern theology, the term heaven seems to signify the eternal state, but that has always seemed strange to me. I would prefer to call the eternal state such things as "the new heavens and new earth," "the new earth," "the new world," "the new creation," or "the eternal state."

The Intermediate State/Afterlife—sometimes referred to as "paradise" in biblical literature. This is the place where people go in between the present and the future coming of Christ. The intermediate state is not the ultimate destination for believers. Our immediate "afterlife" as Christians is not the new creation with the new heavens and new earth. While individuals in paradise are filled with bliss, there is still a sense of waiting for the eternal state to commence. For the believer and the non-believer, it is a much different experience in different realms.

The Eternal State—as this pertains to believers, it is the final, eternal dwelling place of God with His people. This is commonly spoken of as the subject of heaven, and it contains the arrival of the new heavens and new earth and every blessing that comes to fruition with that change. In this book, the phrase new creation is shorthand for describing the eternal state.

Jesus—Jesus has many names/titles that can be appellations of His proper name. In the book of Revelation, He is predominately referred to as the "Lamb." He is also the "Lion," which connects Him to the Lion of Judah motif. Revelation also calls Jesus the "Alpha and the Omega" and the "King of kings and Lord of lords." However, some common biblical titles for Him include "Son of God"—emphasizing His ontological, royal identity as the prince of creation; "Christ/Messiah"—emphasizing His functional role as the promised Messianic Savior; "Lord"—taken from the same Greek word that was translated "Yahweh" in the Old Testament, and which emphasizes His preexistence as the great "I AM." This title is arguably the most explicit of Jesus's deity and identifies Him as the divine ruler of the cosmos and the King of His people. Understanding the identity and role of Jesus is like looking at a mosaic; the individual portraits are to be appreciated, particularly how they make up the whole when they are pieced together. In the same way, no title of Jesus can encapsulate everything about His person or worth—they all need to be appreciated individually for what they communicate, and then placed side-by-side with the rest of christological terminology to form a larger, more accurate depiction of our Messianic King.

Conclusion

If you are reading this, take heart. This book was written in such a way that a scholar could appreciate it, but it is also geared toward the lay Christian who is looking to learn more about the overarching theme of new creation in the Bible. In other words, I wrote this for those who are curious Christians, ready to engage this topic more seriously manner. My desire is hopefully to open your eyes to something far more explanatory of Scripture, and far more beautiful than anything you ever have imagined when it comes to the topic of eschatology!

I encourage you as to read along to examine all Scripture passages that are being discussed. All quotations from Scripture are from the Lexham English Bible (LEB), unless specified differently. I invite you to press forward in this endeavor, ready to meditate further on what you may already know and to learn things that you do not yet know.

Get ready to enter the strange and exciting world of apocalyptic literature. Your imagination will be stimulated. Your convictions will be challenged. And your soul will be strengthened. I hope you are half as excited as I am! However, before we dive into the apocalypse, let us go back to the beginning before humanity fell into sin and despair. Therefore, it is to Garden in Gen 1–3 that we must begin our journey. It is here that we seek to better set the stage of *eschatology* (final things) in light of *protology* (first things).

1

Less Like a Home, More Like a Train

> "Go back?" he thought. "No good at all! Go sideways? Impossible! Go forward? Only thing to do! On we go!"[1]
> —J. R. R. Tolkien's *The Hobbit*

IT IS FASCINATING to me how obsessed everyone is with purpose; yet hardly anyone can answer the question that precedes it, the question of meaning. We cannot understand what God intends for us to do until we first understand what we mean to Him. Yes, meaning, properly comprehended, fuels purpose like blood flowing through veins. And so, if we truly want to gather the most from our study on eschatology, we have to start by getting a grasp on some key things regarding protology (first things). Here is where the question of meaning is answered (at least in part), and where we also discover the moment humanity's meaning went awry.

Why Did God Create Everything?

> "In the beginning, God created the heavens and the earth." (Gen 1:1)

What is the first attribute of God we glean from this verse? Every time I ask this, I get the same answer: "Creator! God is Creator!" Yes! That is a true statement; but it is the wrong answer to the

---

[1] J. R. R. Tolkien, *The Hobbit*, (Boston; New York: Houghton Mifflin Harcourt; Mariner Books, 2012), 66.

question. That is not the first theological truth we learn about God. Let me help you by inflecting a part of this verse.

"In the beginning, God"—Stop there! God simply is. Before there was anything (well, at least in terms of how we understand "anything"), God exists. If you claim to have quite the imagination, I dare you to try to picture what everything was like before there was anything. Imagine the life of God before creation as we know it.

The starting point for all theology is the foundational understanding that God is. The book of Exodus plays on this truth when God reveals to Moses what His name is. God's name is Yahweh, which probably clarifies nothing for you on a purely cursory read. But the Hebrew name is a play on words. "Yahweh" etymologically means "to be." That is why we sometimes refer to God as the "I AM," because that is what His name means. He is who He is, and He is the only one who can make such a claim! He is self-existent; dependent on no one; unrivaled; unique in every way. He is the source of all else. Yahweh is the I AM. Therefore, God simply is.

We need to understand this because God does not need anything—He is self-sufficient. On the contrary, humans are used to actions being derived from some sort of self-gratifying motivation. Hardly ever—if ever—are we motivated purely by altruistic motives. This is not a knock against your character, it is just the result of our lack of self-sufficiency. We have needs, and that is okay. But God is without needs, and whatever He does He does from a completely different motive.

Are you starting to see how amazing this is?

So, what did this self-existent; self-sufficient; completely satisfied being do with His infinite power? He "created the heavens and the earth," which is a somewhat cumbersome way of saying, "He created everything!" From the most microbial life on earth to the most distant star, He made it all! The Hebrew verb "created" (bārā') highlights God's unique creative power and His creatio ex nihilo! Consequently, in the Gen 1:1 bārā' refers exclusively to God as the agent of creation.

The creation of "the heavens and the earth" simply means the creation of the cosmos. (The reference to the creation of the cosmos will be important later in our study; for now, consider this a foreshadowing of future events). I would argue that Gen 1:1 functions as a summary statement for the events of Gen 1–2. It is undoubtedly part of "Day 1" of creation, but it is also a succinct affirmation of *creatio ex nihilo*. God creates everything, and *then* begins to form everything.[2]

Here is where we are so far: creation presents a wise Creator who gives ontological existence for no other purpose but to love and be loved. Yes, that is the purpose—love. We love out of necessity; God loves out of liberty. He does not receive our love to fulfill a need He is otherwise void of. We receive His love because we have a void a billion galaxies could never fulfill without His love. This is essential to the conversation of meaning.

God's creation is an act of love evidenced by Him needing absolutely nothing. Since He is utterly perfect, the only possible outcome that can occur come from creating everything is the possibility of frustration. However, what if God knows something we are not privy to? What if creation was an act of sharing what He has within Himself? What if He wanted to create creatures that in some way reflected or imaged Him, while being able to be in relationship with Him? It is questions like these that only Christian theology, with its articulation of the triune nature of God, can adequately answer.

God is Love Because God is Triune

Perhaps one of the most recognized propositions about the nature of God is found in 1 John 4:8, where the author emphatically remarks that "God is love." The triune God of the Bible is the only

---

[2] It is my belief that we need to stop reading the creation story as a scientific account and start reading it as what it is, a poem of the story of everything! Sadly, in the English text it is easy to miss this nuance. In the Hebrew, the whole creation narrative is one elaborate poem. For further study on this, see the works of John Goldingay, *Old Testament Theology: Israel's Gospel*, vol. 1 (Westmont: IVP Academic, 2003), 871.

Matthews puts it this way: "The passage is doxological as well as didactic, hymnic as well as history." K. A. Mathews, *Genesis 1-11:26*, NAC (Nashville: Broadman & Holman Publishers, 1996), 113.

God of any religion who can genuinely be the essence of love. No other "God" of any other religion can make such a claim. When we say, "God is love," we are saying that love belongs to God's ontology (His nature, essence, or being). We are saying that there has never been a time when God has been devoid of the very essence and embodied definition of love. Allow me to elaborate on this with two scenarios.

In the first scenario, God is unitarian and has eternally existed alone. God is one divine essence and the only person possessing that essence. At some point in eternity God created the angels and the realm of heaven. Sometime later he created the universe, world, and humanity. God acts lovingly towards his creation.

In summary, God adopted the characteristic of love and became the perfect embodiment of it. However, God was not always the essence of love because one cannot be (ontologically) love without having an object to share that love with or act lovingly towards. Thus, God adopted the characteristic of love after his creation. As such, this rules out the Muslim god, Allah, along with and the unitarian god as described by the Jehovah's Witnesses from being able to make the claim of being "love."

In our second scenario, God is triune and has existed in loving community and fellowship from eternity past—one divine essence shared between three distinct persons. God (the Father), the Lord (Jesus), and the Holy Spirit share in the very essence of love and act in love towards one another. Out of love, God created all things with the purpose to glorify Himself and to share His joy with his creation. Because God is love, he acts lovingly towards his creation.

God in His essence is a God of love, and He acts lovingly because He has eternally shared and experienced that love within the Godhead. Each person of the Trinity has been both the object and benefactor of love received and love given.

What, then, can we glean from Gen 1 in light of Christian theology? Sheer delight was the blueprint that birthed creation. Out of liberty, not obligation, God created the cosmos and all creatures. What a beautiful story! While this does not explain everything regarding the creation narrative of Gen 1–2, it does get us on the right track. The triune God created everything for the pure motive of joy. Our supreme meaning is that we are loved and delighted in *just because*.

In light of this, I intend to teach my son to learn this meaning through a mantra that I already speak over him:

> God loves you because He loves you;
> His love is circular in its rhyme and reason.
> His love has no beginning and no end;
> Steadfast and true through every season.

When we grasp this truth, I believe it has the power to change how we approach the whole story of Scripture. We are God's treasure, fashioned by the hands of the happiest craftsman, who imprinted His very image into us when He formed us.

Now, God does not create image-bearers to do nothing with the gift of existence. He invites us into the thrill of being part of His family. Think about it this way, God is one who always has an adventure to share. The first adventure He tasked humanity with was in Eden. It is in the Garden where things get interesting, because my bet is that some of the things discussed below will first shock you, and then, upon further consideration, produce multiple "light bulb moments," which will contribute to our study of eschatology and the goal of the biblical narrative.

Was Eden "Perfect"?

Most people have an overly romantic view of Eden. Adjectives like "perfect" are frequently used to describe Eden before the fall. Phrases like, "Everything was perfect, and then humanity ruined it," are often uttered by Christians. But was Eden actually *perfect*? We are justified in acknowledging the goodness of Eden. However, Eden was not intended to be viewed as the perfected and permanent state. (This should be obvious in light of the events of Gen 3.) Likewise, Eden was not the eschaton. In other words, Eden was never humanity's final and highest state of potential—it was never our final destination. Our goal is not to return to Eden, despite what many preachers may say.

There is a problem if we assume that "sinless" means "perfect." This is a crucial nuance we must be willing to embrace. If we communicate Eden as being "perfect," we must also defend Eden as the ideal form of both human and cosmological existence. If anything can surpass the excellency of Eden, then we must concede that Eden, while very good, still had a progressive destiny.

Furthermore, if salvation is simply a "return to the garden," how can we have assurance that we will not repeat the fatal mistake of our first parents? What will make the new creation superior to Eden? Well, that will take quite a few chapters to unpack. We start with this: Eden was not *perfect*, but it had eschatological *potential*.

From the opening pages of the Bible, it is apparent that God is working toward something more, something better, something *new*. New creation is the goal of the biblical narrative from even the first moment of creation.

No one, not even Adam, has lived in the final existence intended by God for humanity. You read that correctly. Even before the fall, Eden needed a Messiah. As provocative as that sounds, it is biblically true. Not even Adam and Eve had seen life in its fullest potential. Let me say it even more confrontationally: Not even those who are currently in heaven have seen the final aim of creation!

Allow me to open your eyes to the Eden you have never known. A place of wonder, but also warfare. A place that was *sinless*, but not *serpent-less*. A place brimming with eschatological *potential*, but short of perfection. Welcome to the jungle, my friends.

A Garden that Needed Guarding

When God breathed life into Adam, He created him amid a cosmic construction site. Yes, Eden was a work in progress! While Eden was a flourishing garden, the surrounding world was chaotic and in need of subduing. Adam and Eve were to be God's agents in making the rest of the world look like Eden. Humanity, made in the image of God (Gen 1:26), was born with a missional mandate.

In the garden, one tree was deemed off-limits—the tree of knowledge of good and evil, while the second was placed on temporal probation—the tree of life. The tree of knowledge of good and evil was a sacrament of humanity's dependence on God. The tree of life was a sacrament of the higher form of life. Think about it this way: the original mandate for humanity did not represent the eternal mandate. Again, we are talking about a construction site, where the "work" that is to be done during construction is different than the "work" that is enjoyed once the edifice is built.

Here is a key observation: Eden was not a static state. It would be impossible for Adam and Eve's existence to continue in the way Eden had been created. God's original commission of Adam in Gen 2:15 was to "cultivate and keep" Eden. The call to cultivate implied the nurturing and expansion of Eden. The second word, "keep," is a very interesting word because it denotes the task of guarding or protecting something; it is even used in military contexts when something needed guarding against an invading enemy. Immediately we realize Adam was submitted to a test, where an intruder threatened the current progress and the future potential of humanity and creation. So, Eden was not only a cosmic construction site, it was also a spiritual warzone.

But who is the mysterious enemy threatening the idyllic peace and progressive flourishing of Eden? In Gen 3, the antagonist is revealed in the form of a serpent. This serpent, who had rebelled against the Lord, had come to desecrate God's good world. To inherit the tree of life, Adam and Eve needed to slay the serpent and remain faithful to God. The trajectory of creation hinged upon the outcome of Adam and Eve's leading. This is fundamental to the whole Bible. God has always held creation's destiny in conjunction with the cooperation and participation of His human family. Thus, the resurrected creation will only come into full effect when the redeemed people of God are brought into resurrected reality, too (cf. Rom 8:18–23). Resurrection is the hope of both redeemed humanity and physical creation.

The results of Adam and Eve's disobedience in Eden were catastrophic. They were defeated by the serpent—not through combat, but through deception (see Gen 3:1–7). Their partaking in the prohibited tree of knowledge of good and evil demonstrated that their love for God lacked maturity, and the severity of their willful rebellion could not be more exaggerated.

Instead of looking to God alone to grow in the knowledge of good and evil, humanity took a fatal detour, looking to alternative routes, as if there were any other way besides God's way. Anything opposed to the path of life is a path of death, no matter how slight the deviation. Humanity deteriorates when it seeks autonomy. There is no true life apart from God—when all along we were meant to be creatures dependent on our Creator. We will never graduate from our dependency on God, and any thought otherwise is a seed of sinful deception.

The First Sin

Adam, and thereby humanity's circumstances in the garden, present to us God's heart in establishing relationship with us: that of a willful choice of love. God did not create people to be emotionless, soulless robots. He could have programmed us like a computer to perform a specific set of functions, but that was not His choice. Because God desires our love and affection, He gives us the capacity to have volition and agency to respond to His love. This is different than calling it "free will," which has its faults (by definition). We have a *will* that is capable of and responsible for its own choices, but as opposed to it being "free," it is meant to be responsive to God's determined design. We are not talking about God creating humanity with a call to do as they please with their inherent freedom. On the contrary, being created in His image must also imply that there is a way in which the image-bearer relates to the One it images. If we image God, then He becomes the exemplar of how our choices are to be patterned after. The character of God becomes the wisdom that shapes our ethical decisions, which is a helpful segue back into our discussion of the fall.

We are made with the highest dignity imaginable, created in the very image and likeness of our Creator (Gen 1:26–27), and in light of this God gave humanity the quintessential test of love. Through the unexplained and mysterious prohibition to abstain from the fruit of the tree of knowledge of good and evil, God proposed a question of covenantal relationship to humanity: "Do you trust Me?"

God was demanding that Adam and Eve give Him their unrivaled allegiance and affection. The archetypal sin of humanity was not one of pride, selfishness, or ignorance. It was not a sinful desire to be like God, for humanity was *already* like God, made in His image (again, Gen 1:26–27; cf. Col 3:10). Nevertheless, it is noteworthy that the serpent's cunning was, in part, based on making Adam and Eve forget who they already were and who they were becoming.

Ignorance is unable to vindicate our first parents, as they were instructed to not eat of that tree. God was not required to explain the reasoning for His command; He deserves our loyal trust despite our knowing, or not knowing, all the details. You could say that the details were part of Adam and Eve's discipleship deficit. Discipleship is about "following" the leading of the Lord through the gap of our knowledge deficit and God's wisdom. The transmission of His wisdom into our hearts takes time, trust, and obedience in the steps in-between.

The first sin is also the root from which all sin sprouted. It is the grave notion of thinking there is an alternative to absolute devotion to God alone. This is a step further than monotheistic worship; this is "God-*onlyism*."[3] Said another way: There is no other way than God's way, and any other way is detrimental to the design and potential of humanity and creation.

The moment when Adam and Eve sinned took place prior to the bite of the forbidden fruit. The fatal moment of sin occurred the moment the serpent cunningly led Adam and Eve to believe that total allegiance to God was not the *only* option. The achievement of knowledge of good and evil is not in and of itself evil; instead, it is *how* that knowledge is achieved which makes it good or bad. Adam and Eve snatched that knowledge on their own, apart from God.

God was not holding out on Adam and Eve; He was simply taking them through a courtship process of love and growth. They would go through gradual stages of progress and, with their

---

3 I am indebted to Pastor Wayne Kinde, a great friend and mentor, for all the magnificent conversations we have had pertaining to this point (i.e., the cosmology and eschatology of Gen 1–3).

growth, the graduation of original creation to its higher form. But that is not what we see. Instead, Adam and Eve sought to discover good and evil on their own terms—saying to God: "We can rule this world without you." This is simply not true! Humanity ruling apart from God is what we can chalk up to the twentieth century being the bloodiest century in recorded human history! Yet, it also misses the main point. Ruling the world righteously misses the end goal if it is ruling apart from God. Do we not see that God created us for relationship with Him? As will become more apparent, the concept of relationship with God will be an important concept as we flesh out future chapters.

Returning to the garden, we must ask one important question: does God understand the difference between good and evil? He does, but not in the same manner that Adam and Eve, and consequently their progeny, do. Adam and Eve learned the knowledge of good and evil by experience. They had experienced good, and then by snatching the forbidden fruit, they felt the reality of evil—they learned sin, experientially.

God knows evil, but not through experience. His knowledge of evil is one of observation or intellectual sense. He has observed the fallen spiritual beings (epitomized by the serpent), and now fallen humanity chose to do what is antithetical to what is good. Goodness is that which stems from God's very character and heart. Adam and Eve could have learned what evil was by listening to God and learning it at an intellectual level without ever having to learn it *experientially*, and by doing so, they could have experienced much more of the goodness of God. However, the test of love revealed the distrust that the image-bearers had for their Creator.

Nevertheless, we cannot point the finger as if Adam and Eve are isolated culprits. We, too, have willfully chosen sin. Surely, we were born into a sinful world with spiritually marred DNA. Adam and Eve have passed on the condition of sin, but the guilt of sin humanity acquired on its own without any help. Nevertheless, our choices reveal our depravity stemming from the first sin. The serpent has infected us all, and so we all need a Messiah to slay the serpent that resides in the hearts of humanity.

Prior to the act of sin, there is always the initial root of temptation that distracts our attention away from goodness and toward rebellion. This distraction is described in the book of James, where James notes that "each one is tempted when he is dragged away and enticed by his own desires. Then desire, after it has conceived, gives birth to sin, and sin, when it is brought to completion, gives birth to death" (Jas 1:14–15). All sin stems from entertaining the thought that there is another way other than the way of the Lord. The moment we think there is another option is the very moment we are headed towards the destructive path of sin and away from the blessing.

Perhaps this would be a good time to remark that the Hebrew concept of sin is to "miss the mark." It is likened to shooting an arrow at a target but not hitting it precisely where you wanted. Any deviation, great or small, is a miss. But sin is not like a playful game of archery, it is far more deadly to humans.

Sin is anything described as antagonistic to God's design, screaming through our actions that we not only believe we *know* better than God, but that we *love* something more than Him. To put it simply, sin is the fundamental problem in the world.

A Place of Probation and Potential

Upon a careful reading of Gen 1–3, you will notice that Adam and Eve had yet to graduate from their probationary testing. They had yet to be awarded the privilege to eat of the tree of life, otherwise, they would have obtained immortal life "and live forever" (Gen 3:22). Eden contained both the test of love (from God) and the genuine threat of warfare (from the serpent). And no matter how you look it, humanity failed its test and thus plunged all of creation into a world marred by sin.

After the entrance of sin into the world, the tree of life was restricted and kept away from Adam and Eve (Gen 3:22–24). The fruit of the tree of life could not be consumed by them or by their offspring. For humanity to eat from the tree of life would only further the chaos that sin introduced into the world by granting eternal life to God's enemies. It would have been utterly disastrous for our first parents to achieve immortality in their sinful state. Death acts as a restraint of sin by limiting the enduring life of sinners.

Cosmologically, Gen 1–3 shows Eden as a place of probation—a place where fidelity was tested. The tree of life serves as a sacramental sign of the immortality and glory to be granted to humanity upon the condition of perfect obedience, of which Adam failed. The gift of immortality and the ever-increasing joy of knowing God intimately was tarnished, at least for the moment.

But God did not give up on humanity. While we were exiled from Eden, we were not forsaken. The great irony is that after the first sin it was Adam and Eve who hid from God, not the other way around. Sin has indeed separated us from God, but the stiff-arm of rejection does not come from the divine arm. Humanity is responsible for the walls of hostility erected against God. He only intends to win us back to Himself, cure us of our wayward hearts, and elevate our relationship with Him to the highest status imaginable. And so, God is giving us an invitation to trust Him. Because faith, understood biblically, is like signing a waiver that grants God permission to have His way with our hearts. After all, we all know we need more than heart surgery, we need a "new heart" (Ezek 36:26) that comes from a new covenant.

Preconsummate Stage

The tree of life plays a pivotal role in biblical cosmology. It is a vibrant picture of vitality and freshness, without any hint of decay. And while we confess that God is the ultimate source of life, who is both its creator and sustainer, the tree of life is God's symbolic, tactile aesthetic representation of this truth.

Furthermore, not only does the tree of life communicate life unending, but the tree is also a symbol of intimate solidarity with God. The tree likewise demonstrates that humanity is totally dependent upon God, even while existing in a sinless condition. However, at the fall the tree of life was delimited, resulting in the loss of any chance of immortal life for Adam and Eve. A once intimate relationship with God was now in utter ruins.

As we have noted, the serpent's presence in the garden made God's construction site into a turf war to see whose kingdom humanity would participate in building. A non-stop battle with the serpent is not the ideal state of humanity's eternal residence. Likewise, the presence of the tree of knowledge of good and evil, with its attached promise of demise, was a continual reminder of God's one command for Adam and Eve and the looming death that awaited them if they took up and ate of the fruit.

Eden was "very good," and it had the eschatological potential to graduate to God's intended perfection—the new heavens and the new earth. Sadly, it never lived up to this potential. Sin derailed humanity from entering eternal glory, and along with it, disrupted the escalation of all of creation into eternal glory as well. Therefore, with this one act of rebellion, we are presented with the storyline of the Bible.

In order to understand eschatology, and with it the story of Scripture, we must refrain from an overly romanticized view of Eden, one that views the garden as the perfect and the final existence of humanity. Although Eden was created in a sinless state, it was nevertheless still incomplete; it still needed consummation. Similarly, the condition of God's image-bearers was in a state of wavering. Will humanity trust God and receive immortality, or will it rebel against God and be subjugated to death? You could say that life and death was hanging in the balance at Eden—and it all came down to one Shakespearean dilemma of epic proportions: to eat, or not to eat.

The pre-consummate stage in Eden still needed to reach the completed and irreversible stage. In light of this, ponder the following five primary conditions that needed to be addressed before immortal life could be secured:

1. Victory over the presence of evil (by defeating the serpent and his followers).
2. Ultimate security against committing sin (the inner transformation of the heart).
3. The gift of immortality (by partaking of the tree of life and having union with the source of life, God).

4. Ever-present vitality so as to prevent creation from decaying (ushering in the new heavens and new earth, with its unending newness of life).
5. Heightened privileges regarding humans' relationship with the triune God (which will be explained later in this book).

The existence of these conditions does not undermine God's sovereignty. For reasons that are far beyond human comprehension, God is bringing humanity to the highest aim of new creation, knowing that the fall would be part of the process. Ultimately, God is sovereign over all circumstances, and we see that, despite the pathway to get there, God is working all things toward the perfect eternal state—a resurrected cosmos.

It is only in Christ that we can obtain the tree of life with all its blessings. Thus, in His message to the church of Ephesus in Rev 2, Jesus grants believers who endure until the end permission to eat from the tree of life as a reward. He is, in essence, offering eschatological life beyond probation, even beyond Eden (cf. Rev 2:7).

And that is exactly what we will explore in the following chapters.

The Promised Eternal State

New creation has been the grand objective ever since the original creation. Genesis 1-2 presents us a project site, not a finished one. As N. T. Wright notes, " ... even the glorious world of Genesis 1 was the beginning of something, rather than an end in itself. It was itself a great signpost, pointing to the world that God always intended to make out of it."[4]

That is worth repeating. *Eden is more like a signpost rather than the hallmark of our destination.* The final and highest hope of a Christian is *Edenic*, but it is not *Eden* (at least as it was in the original creation). As you read on, you will come to discover that the aim of our hope is more like a new, escalated Eden.

Our journey in studying the doctrine of new creation in the book of Revelation has begun with our acknowledgment of the

---

4 N. T. Wright, *Revelation for Everyone* (Louisville: Westminster John Knox, 2015), 198.

need for new creation. There is no way to go backward; in fact, Eden was not meant to be the final destination. So, we must press forward in God's redemptive plan.

An analogy will help you sink your teeth into what I am getting at here. Think of heaven not as a *home*, but as a *train*. A home is stationary, its foundations planted firmly in place. By contrast, a train is mobile, freely able to move between destinations.

Part of the problem is that few Christians have been introduced to the distinction between the present heaven, sometimes called the "intermediate state," and the future heaven, sometimes called the "eternal state." (As stated in the Introduction, we would do better to refer to the future of heaven as new creation.) When I talk about the present, intermediate condition of heaven, I use the term, *heaven* just for the sake of familiarity.

When I discuss the future, eternal, redeemed state that will be ushered in when Jesus returns, I call this the "new creation" because that is the fulfillment of God's eschatological ("end goal") promise.

The plan is not to *evacuate* earth to heaven, but to invade and pervade earth with heaven! The new creation is nothing short of the reality of heaven infiltrating all creation down to the smallest minutia of the human soul.

If the current state of heaven was to be the final place for believers, where the journey of God's people terminates, then the story of the Bible would be unfinished and incomplete. The opening of Gen 1–2 narrates the creation of the heavens and earth; the closing chapters of Rev 21–22 proclaim the promised new heaven and new earth. God did not give up on His creation; that is not His character. God's plan not only will redeem, but it will also escalate the condition of everything to its highest form, far beyond our comprehension.

Heaven is less like a home and more like a train. Heaven is headed toward a collision course with our world. The two worlds—God's realm and our realm—are meant to collide and become one. The train is coming home to earth! This is good news for a depressed and degrading world. This is the gospel that the Messianic King, Jesus, came to proclaim and enact.

To be crystal clear: there are two wrong notions of eschatology that our exposition of the biblical text will rectify. The first one is the notion that Eden represented God's perfect state of existence, and if it was not for the fall, humanity would have continued dwelling in Eden in the static state it was in.

However, such a representation of Eden is not that is not what we find in Scripture. As I have argued, there are explicit clues in the text that push against any reading of Eden existing in a permanent or a perfected state. Again, it is better to consider Eden as a construction zone with hostile intruders trying to foil the plan. Though the work of the gospel reverses the curse, it does not imply that our aim is to return to Eden. The reversal of the curse gets us back on track to what was started in Eden. The Edenic ideal and vision—what I call the new creation or resurrected cosmos—was always about escalating creation to a higher form of life, even beyond Eden. You could say that the escalated Eden is the goal of eschatology.

The second wrong notion that we must rectify is the far more common one, that heaven is the final home for believers. While no passage in the Bible states this, somehow Church history has come to communicate this as if this is the clear-cut gospel message. Heaven is important, but it is not the apex of ambition from God's perspective. The point is not to watch this fallen world implode as we are raptured away to heaven. Returning once again to the analogy above, heaven is like a train moving towards its final destination. The kingdom of heaven is on the move, breaking through the fabric of our reality even now, yet it also remains a future expectation of immense and pervasive fulfillment, where heaven and earth will no longer be separate entities.

From here, having refreshed our minds on the drama of Scripture that began in Gen 1–3, we turn our focus now to the book of Revelation. At this point, I trust that our understanding of the story of the Bible is sufficient enough to make the jump from the garden to the apocalyptic drama of Revelation. If this seems like too much of a leap, perhaps a return refresher on the story of Scripture between Genesis and Revelation would help reorient our understanding.

And so, we press on with our thinking in order to correspond with what God is sovereignly doing as He ushers in the new creation through our inaugurated experience. We must also anticipate and have a biblical view of hope as we look forward to the future eschatological consummation of everything being made new in the promised eternal state—a resurrected cosmos. The train is in motion, and in the words of Tolkien, "On we go!"

2

The Emerald Throne

> *Worship is praise in response to God's revelation of himself.*[1]
> —Richard D. Phillips

IF I WERE TO KNOCK on your door, you would probably answer it, and you might even invite me inside. Unless you are a person of some notoriety and public influence, most people do not have security protocol preventing strangers from knocking on their doors. For example, if I attempted to go to the White House unannounced, I would be detained by Secret Service agents before I could even get a glimpse of the front door. The president of the United States is not an individual who takes impromptu guests. Meeting with such a powerful and influential person is almost always by invitation only.

We begin this chapter with an obvious observation—no one can go knocking on the door to God's throne. This is an element to His transcendence. Western Christianity has perhaps overemphasized God's accessibility at the expense of His holy transcendence. Only by being summoned can a person, quite literally, enter into His manifest presence.

In Rev 4:1, Jesus Himself summoned John to the throne room of God. The throne was always seen as the central focal point in Jewish thought. Being consistent with its roots, Revelation is structured to show the throne of God as a focal point of the book. The

---

[1] Richard D. Phillips, *Reformed Expository Commentary: Revelation* (New Jersey: P&R Publishing Company, 2017), 181.

word "throne" (*thronos*) is used a total of sixty-two times in the entire New Testament, forty-seven of which occur in Revelation alone. Clearly, Revelation wants to disclose something that is usually beyond our vantage point.

Behind the Scenes

In his vision in Rev 4, John gets a look behind the scenes—the view from heaven despite the chaotic turmoil happening on earth. The seven churches in Asia Minor all were experiencing varying degrees of persecution. There were dangerous times, when identifying as a Christian could cost a person their life.

Thus, part of the reason for John's in Rev 4 vision was to encourage his audience by reminding them of who sat on the throne—the throne that really counts! It is here in Revelation that the reader gets a glimpse of God's vantage point and peeks into God's throne room as it appears in the present condition.

The sporadic imagery is not meant to give us a tour of the throne room. Instead, it is meant to communicate something about God's majesty. This type of apocalyptic imagery is quite common in related Jewish literature. One needs only to be reminded of Isaiah's vision of God's glory in the temple (Isa 6), or Ezekiel's angelic encounter (Ezek 1-2), or Daniel's vision of the four beasts (Dan 7). The author of Revelation is using imagery that would be easily recognizable for Jewish readers who were well familiar with Jewish literature of those days.

This is no subtle vision, however. As one cohesive scene, Rev 4-5 provides the interpretative key to understanding the totality of the book of Revelation. It is my belief that it's more vital to camp out in Rev 4-5 instead of focusing on the various details of chapters 6-20. If we misunderstand these chapters, we run the risk of missing the message of the book of Revelation as a whole.

In these early chapters of Revelation, John is transported to another dimension in order to receive a vision. The vision that John receives is meant to comfort his readers and provide them with an understanding of events occurring on earth from a theocentric lens. Meaning, when we see what is going on through heaven's vantage point, we are more likely to have an understanding that produces endurance in the present moment, even when things are extremely difficult.

This is significant because Revelation is an unveiling that guides the reader to an understanding of past events, such as the death and resurrection of Jesus; present events pertaining to the latter first-century audience; and future events like the return of Christ and the ushering in of the new creation. In light of this, eschatology is best grasped when the whole picture from past, present, and future is brought together.

John's vantage point is not as most people would think of it. It is not that John was teleported somewhere far out among the stars to a place with pearly gates and a sign that says "heaven." Most westerners have a wrong concept of heaven and earth. Heaven (unfortunately) is typically viewed as immaterial and spiritual, while the earth is physical and generally has bad or evil connotations.

The reality is that heaven and earth are intimately related and interlocked. Heaven and earth are separated by *dimension*, not galaxies.

N. T. Wright also comes to a similar conclusion, noting that "'Heaven,' God's sphere of reality, is right here, close beside us, intersecting with our ordinary reality. It is not so much like a door opening high up in the sky, far away. It is more like a door opening right in front of us where before we could only see this room, this field, this street."[2] He goes on to say, "[John's vision] is about a prophet being taken into God's throne room so that he can see 'behind the scenes' and understand both what is going to take place and how it all fits together and makes sense."[3] And so, we enter the text of Rev 4.

World of Color

After these things I looked, and behold, an open door in heaven, and the former voice that I had heard like a trumpet

---

2 N. T. Wright, *Revelation for Everyone*, (Louisville: Westminster John Knox, 2015), 42..

3 Wright, *Revelation for Everyone*, 43.

speaking with me was saying, "Come up here and I will show you the things which must take place after these things." Immediately I was in the Spirit, and behold, a throne was set in heaven, and one was seated on the throne. And the one seated was similar in appearance to jasper and carnelian stone, and a rainbow was around the throne similar in appearance to emerald. (Rev 4:1–3)

When was the last time you were lost in wonder? When was the last time you were baffled beyond belief? Many would concur that we have lost our sense of imagination. Maybe the constant exposure to technology caused our brains to be less creative. However, one of the most remarkable things about the Bible is its ability to help us reclaim what we have lost. As we open the pages of Revelation our imaginations are instantly stirred, and any loss of wonder that we may have experienced comes rushing back as we are gripped by the symbolism that pervades the great apocalyptic jewel of the New Testament.

It goes without saying that reading the book of Revelation is far from boring. Though it may be confusing at times, it is simultaneously full of encouragement as well. Understanding Revelation as it was meant to be understood is not only part of our due diligence in studying Scripture, it also allows us to share in the same astonishment that John experienced on Patmos when he was visited by the resurrected Christ.

I enjoy being in wonder. At Disneyland's California Adventure there is one of the most impressive attractions I have ever seen: *World of Color*. For over twenty minutes a spectacular production is displayed for hundreds of viewers. The water in the middle of the hub of California Adventure sprouts upward with various colors dancing to the music playing over the speakers. Clips of famous Disney movie scenes are played, and the lights, water, and even flames of fire correspond to the music. It is easy to lose track of time while entranced by such a spectacle. The vibrant colors are marvelous. The sights, the sounds, the whole experience is memorable for kids and adults alike.

As I study Rev 4, I cannot help but think of the *World of Color* experience at Disneyland. I can bet with confidence that God's throne room—with its colors, lights, sounds, and grandeur—is far superior to any production Disney can put on. Although John only gives us a brief description, we have to believe that God can far surpass Disney in stimulating awe.[4] And our imaginations are challenged to think of such wonder.

Chapter four of Revelation opens with a vivid description of the appearance of the "one seated on the throne" (4:2). However, John's depiction of the risen Christ is not what we would expect. As finite beings trying to portray the infinite to other finite beings, we are at the disposal of simile, metaphor, analogy, and symbolism. We lack a proper vocabulary, so we are left with using "like" language to describe the indescribable. As will become overtly apparent at the outset, Revelation is not lacking in its use of vibrant and otherworldly language to describe God and His angelic hosts. Welcome to apocalyptic literature!

Indulge me for a moment, if you will. Imagine you are speaking to someone who has never seen snow before. How would you describe it to them? What sort of examples would you use to try and explain what is for them an unknown element? Now, try to empathize with John as he endeavors to communicate a vision of God's glorious throne to finite beings who not only have never seen it, but who can hardly even picture such infinite majesty.

In Rev 4, John was attempting to describe the glory of God to readers lacking categories for such an experience. The best he can do is describe God's appearance with the colors of precious stones. Jasper refers to anything of the red, green, or blue variety. Carnelian is a fiery red stone, and most likely reflects God's fierce love and passion.

Much can be said about the personality of God, but He could never be described as stoic or callous. No biblical writer depicts God with such boring or apathetic terminology.

God's throne is also encircled with an emerald rainbow, a dazzling, radiant green color, that reflects the indescribable majesty of the "one on the throne." This sounds a lot like what Ezekiel saw

---

[4] And again, Isa 6 and Ezek 1–2 (thought ancient descriptions) will help demonstrate how humans end up in awe before a revelation of God's throne.

in Ezek 1:27–28, in which there is a world of colorful and glorious light proceeding from God's throne and presence.

Ezekiel's account is reminiscent of the psalmist's confession, "You cover Yourself with light" (Ps 104:2, GNB).[5] The Common English Bible dynamically translates Ps 104:2 as, "You wear light like a robe." Again, the text draws our attention to a God so beautiful, so full of splendor, that He radiates magnificent light around Him. The closest parallel I can identify to describe God's glorious presence is the magnificent auroras that light up the arctic skies. These beautiful light displays dances and sway to music we are unable to hear, as though the skies were alive! If such light displays cause us to lose our breath in wonder, how can we not even more so be in awe of a God whose throne emulates such lavish light? Could it be that our imaginations are far too small, especially when it comes to how we picture God?

The ancient reader would have been drawn into the scene presented in Rev 4 and all its wonder. Our response to John's vision should be no different today. The glory of God is captivating. Not only is this true of His throne and physical appearance, but His character also captivates us. His royal beauty is accompanied by His royal goodness. He is a King who is worthy of worship. For the ancient Hebrew, awe was the highest form of worship. We can learn something here, as most of us do not posture ourselves in such a way as to cultivate greater awe of our God. I believe we need to be seeking that expression of awe as a response to encountering the revelation of who God is.

As I write about God's glory, I am reminded of a song called "Beautiful," by Phil Wickham, that praises the beauty of God. I wish there were more songs like it! There cannot be too many songs written about God's attributes and actions, or His beauty and splendor.

The Throne Room

And around the throne were twenty-four thrones, and seated on the thrones were twenty-four elders dressed in white

---

5 Cf. 1 Tim 6:16.

clothing, and on their heads were gold crowns. And from the throne came out lightnings and sounds and thunders, and seven torches of fire were burning before the throne, which are the seven spirits of God. And before the throne was something like a sea of glass, like crystal, and in the midst of the throne and around the throne were four living creatures full of eyes in front and in back. And the first living creature was similar to a lion, and the second living creature was similar to an ox, and the third living creature had a face like a man's, and the fourth living creature was similar to an eagle flying. And the four living creatures, each one of them, had six wings apiece, full of eyes around and inside, and they do not have rest day and night, saying, "Holy, holy, holy is the Lord God All-Powerful, the one who was and the one who is and the one who is coming! (Rev 4:4–8)

The earth revolves around the sun, not the other way around. In God's reality, all the angels revolve around Him. God is the central focal point of the heavenly throne room, and His throne is the center of the universe. All attention is solely on Him. There is nothing in the throne room worthy of worship other than God alone. Heaven truly is theocentric.

In the description of the throne room quoted above, John introduces to us twenty-four elders. These twenty-four individuals represent a combination of the twelve tribes of Israel and the twelve apostles, which taken a collective whole symbolizes the universal Church. The elders epitomize the people of God who span across both Testaments, both Jews and Gentiles alike.[6] I am persuaded this is the correct designation.

The term for "elders," *presbuterous*, never applies to angels, and thus provides further evidence that these twenty-four individuals represent the redeemed people of God. Therefore, it makes sense for the crown of a conqueror to be given to believers rather than angels. This is the case in Rev 2:10, where the "crown of life" is offered as a reward to all believers who prevail and keep the faith.

---

6 Cf. Ronald Trail, *An Exegetical Summary of Revelation 1–11*, 2nd edition. (Dallas: SIL International, 2008), 121.

In addition to the crown of life, they also are robed in "white garments," which denote ritual purity, having been cleansed and forgiven of sin. After being washed in the blood of the Lamb, believers are ritually pure and free from the stain of sin (Rev 7:14; 22:13–14). These twenty-four elders, then, are redeemed people from both the Old and New Testament (covenant) eras, and they now have begun to receive the rewards promised in the seven letters of Rev 2 and 3.[7]

Out of the throne comes thunder and lightning. The atmospheric phenomena recall the events in recorded in Exod 19:16, where God appeared at Mount Sinai in thunder and lightning and a thick cloud. It is important to note how this phenomenon moves the plot forward in Revelation.

At the conclusion of the seventh seal, John notes that "there were thunders and sounds and lightnings and an earthquake" (Rev 8:5). Similarly, at the end of the seventh trumpet, we read that "there were lightnings and sounds and thunders and an earthquake and large hail" (11:19). Finally, at the end of the seventh bowl, John records that "there were lightnings and sounds and thunders, and there was a great earthquake, as has not happened from the time humanity has been on the earth" (16:18).

The "seven Spirits of God" echo back to Revelation 1:4, where the same phrase appears. Revelation speaks of "seven Spirits" as a way of referring to the fullness of the Holy Spirit. Seven is a number that represents completion, or perfection, in biblical literature; thus, this is speaking of the sevenfold Spirit of God.

Gordon D. Fee comments: "[The seven Spirits of God] is rightly understood as 'the sevenfold Spirit,' imagery taken from Isaiah 11:2, where it said the Messiah will experience 'the Spirit of the Lord' resting on him, who is then described with six Spirit-endowed qualities ('the Spirit of wisdom and understanding,' etc.)."[8]

Another fascinating symbol in Revelation is in reference to the sea. To the ancient Jewish reader, the sea was a place of chaos and

---

7 Note that the eschatological rewards of Rev 2–3 are a mixture of inaugurated rewards presently experienced *and* future rewards that will be realized at the consummation of the kingdom.

8 Gordon D. Fee, *Revelation*, NCCS (Eugene: Cascade Books, 2011), 70–71.

disorder.[9] In contrast, heaven, being God's reality, has a sea, as well. This is not surprising, because Solomon's temple had a sea of bronze (1 Kgs 7:23–26) and it was traditionally thought that Solomon's temple symbolized both Eden and of heaven. For the author of Hebrews, the heavenly sanctuary is a "copy and shadow" of the earthly sanctuary (Heb 8:5; cf. Exod 25:40), which implies that Solomon's earthly temple resembles God's heavenly temple as a microcosm.

God's sanctuary also has a sea, but instead of raging and storming, it is calm and controlled. So tamed is the sea around God's throne that it appears as glass. Picture still water that reflects its surroundings. I think of the lakes in the Pacific Northwest that, when absent of people, are so still that they reflect the mountains and scenery around them. It is a serene experience to be near them. There is clearly something symbolic being communicated here, regardless of whether God literally has a "sea of glass" around His throne.

The most chaotic natural force in our world—the sea—is at ease in God's reality. Richard Bauckham rightly observes that "Heaven is the sphere of ultimate reality: what is true in heaven must become true on earth."[10] This is the final, future fulfillment of the Lord's Prayer found in Matt 6:11. One day the reality of heaven will pervade the reality of earth and chaos will be no more. Such hope should provide comfort to our anxious souls. We can have tranquility as we trust God, who is sovereign over all things. As the "sea" in God's sphere is contained, void of chaos, so God will one day make the same true "on earth as it is in heaven" (Matt 6:11).

The Song Without Cease

> And the four living creatures, each one of them, had six wings apiece, full of eyes around and inside, they do not have rest day and night, saying, "Holy, holy, holy, is the Lord God

---

9 Cf. Job 9:5–14; 26:12; 38:8–11; Pss 65:7; 74:13–14; 77:16; 89:9–10; 104:7; Nah 1:4.

10 Richard Bauckham, *The Theology of the Book of Revelation* (Cambridge: Cambridge University Press, 1993), 31.

All-Powerful, the one who was and the one who is and the one who is coming!'" (Rev 4:8).

This hymn of praise should be viewed not as dry or monotonous, but as a celebration of God that never ceases to amaze us. His majestic holiness and beauty are worthy of a repetitive chorus.

On few occasions I have overheard Christians grumble over the nature of modern worship songs and their aptitude for repetitive lyrics. Such grumbling makes me ponder whether these same people will be bothered by the hymn of praise from the four living creatures in John's vision. Truth be told, some songs are worthy of repetition because the object of the song is worthy of those words ten-thousand-fold!

The Trisagion sung by the four living creatures emphasized the absolute holiness of God. This same outburst of praise is found in Isaiah's encounter with Yahweh in the temple. There, as Isaiah is in utter awe, two Seraphim (literally, "the burning ones") cry out, "Holy, holy, holy is Yahweh of hosts" (Isa 6:1–3). This rare threefold repetition draws remarkable attention to God's ontological uniqueness. His essence is utterly distinct, and there is nothing about Him that is tainted by sin. God's name, reputation, and character are "holy and awesome" (Ps 111:9c).

However, sometimes we interject subjective connotations into the discussion of holiness. For example, we may reserve the word holiness for the "do-gooders" who are morally upright. Or perhaps we limit the concept of holiness to a mere synonym of righteousness. Either way, we limit the sense of holiness and dilute it of its fullness of meaning.

While it certainly is not void of morality, holiness is richer in meaning. Holiness is ethical by implication, but ontological by nature. It is about *being* set apart rather than behaving a certain way. The action is just the by-product of the identity. We are holy in that we are marked with purpose and affection. God is holy in that He is the purpose. He is the *telos*, the summation of everything.

In the Old Testament, no other book has more to say about the holiness of God than the book of Leviticus. It is here that we encounter the most direct and to-the-point directive from God on holiness: "You must be holy, because I, Yahweh your God, *am* holy" (Lev 19:2; cf. 11:44–45). Taken on its own, this is impossible. However, because of our union with Christ, *we are holy*. In fact, we are so much more! As Paul tells the Corinthian believers, because of [God] you are in Christ Jesus, who became to us wisdom from God, righteousness and sanctification and redemption" (1 Cor 1:30).

In translations of the New Testament, the term "holy ones" (*hagioi*) is often rendered as "saints."[11] Thus, Christians are saints who sometimes sin, not sinners who sometimes get it right. The dichotomy of being both a saint and sinner is captured articulately in the popular Latin phrase *simul justus et peccator*, "at the same time justified and sinner." This is a paradox that all believers need to understand. We are a sacred people, touched by divine grace and ambassadors of the realm of God.[12] We can grow in righteousness, for example, but holiness is a status that is given by God.

While we are on a lifelong pursuit of practical holiness, manifested in the moment-by-moment battle against sin, we nevertheless stand already righteous before God based on our union with Christ. Our present status as "holy ones" is purely a divine gift of being joined to Christ. Our union with Christ is an eschatological reality that is in no way affected by the ebb and flow of human emotions. We either *are* holy or we *are not* holy. It is not a comparative term with degrees of difference. We may not always conduct ourselves in congruence with who we are as holy ones, but we nevertheless remain holy because we are united with Christ. Therefore, as long as we remain united to Christ we will always be ontologically and positionally holy. Our moral transformation is simply an outworking of becoming what we already are in Him. And our status as "holy ones" is only because God—the Holy, Holy, Holy One—has declared and prepared us as such (cf. Rom 8:29–30).

---

11 Approximately 61 times the New Testament refers to believers as "saints." Examples include: Rom 1:7; 8:27; 12:13; 15:25, 26; 15:31; 16:15; 1 Cor 1:2; 6:1; 14:33; 16:1, 15; 2 Cor 1:1; 8:4; 9:1, 12; 13:12; Eph 1:1, 5, 18; 2:19; 3:8, 18; 4:12; 5:3; 6:18; Phil 1:1; 4:21, 22; Col 1:2, 4, 26.

12 "Holiness," edited by Douglas Mangum et al., *Lexham Theological Wordbook* (Bellingham: Lexham Press, 2014).

Heaven sings praises of God's holiness. And I can only imagine the quality of musical worship that is taking place there right now: the victorious celebratory songs, the songs that bring you to tears, and everything in between. If our eternal destiny were only to sing the praises of our God, then it would be a glorious destiny nonetheless! Fee powerfully puts into words what I am getting at: "All together this series of images is intended to inspire awe and wonder on the part of the reader, who is being brought into the presence of God, and before whom only awe and worship are the worthy responses."[13]

So, why take the time to explain all of this? The reason is simple: the exposition of Rev 4 is not merely a collection of isolated factoids. What we are suggesting is that Revelation presents heaven (as it is at the time of John's vision) as being a place where its citizens are enthralled with their God. He is so beautiful that the most desired thing to do is adore and enjoy His manifest presence. It should go without saying then that John is not offering an itinerary of the events in heaven. Heaven is much more that a place of dazzling lights and musical worship—this just so happens to be the description John has given for his readers.

Nevertheless, the exposition above will prove useful as this study progresses. As we move forward, we will explore a few other interesting details regarding John's description of heaven, along with an excursus. What we will start to see is that John is developing a scene—Revelation 4 is the setting for Revelation 5. And takes place in the following passages not only provides context for what John sees in heaven, more importantly, the vision inspires us as we continue to live on earth—giving us a vision of what God's eschatological goal is and how He is working toward that—and how He has already begun an integral part of the final sequence of events of human history.

Casting Crowns

And whenever the living creatures give glory and honor and thanks to the one who is seated on the throne, the one who

---

13 Fee, *Revelation*, 71.

lives forever and ever, the twenty-four elders fall down before the one who is seated on the throne and worship the one who lives forever and ever, and put down their crowns before the throne, saying, "You are worthy, our Lord and God, to receive glory and honor and power, because you have created all things, and because of your will they existed and were created." (Rev 4:9–11)

When I was a child, my mother would often give me a coin to toss in a nearby fountain. I was told of the fictional power of the fountain to hear the wishes of the one offering the coin to the enchanted waters. Make a wish, toss the coin in the fountain, and yearn to see your wish come true.

While the coin has inherent value (either five, ten, or twenty-five cents value), I considered paying homage to the fountain of greater value and a more appropriate use for the coin. The childish analogy is merely fun, and I eventually came to realize the inability of the fountain to grant my every wish.

However, crowns are of no insignificant value, especially when God is the giver of such crowns, as is the case in Rev 4. The twenty-four elders "put down," or, according to the translation I favor, "cast their crowns," before God (Rev 4:10 ESV). We have already noted that these elders represent redeemed believers from both the Old and New Testament eras. They have received their crowns probably as a fulfillment of the promise of Rev 2:10, where Jesus said that those who endure "until death" would inherit "the crown of life."

The word for "crowns" comes from the Greek word *stephanos*. It could suggest the victor's wreath given for winning an athletic event, or a crown that a person of royalty would wear. The imagery, I believe, is twofold and most likely refers to both.

These crowns represent a symbol of the eschatological rewards for the overcomer (Rev 2:10; 3:11; cf. Jas 1:12; 1 Pet 5:4). Those who adorn these crowns will experience God's victory, blessing, and the totality of eternal life as the reward for persevering amidst a hostile world.

It is remarkable that John does not refer to any significant Old

Testament characters among the twenty-four elders. Certainly we would expect such giants of the faith like Abraham, Moses, David, or even Paul to be among this elite group of saints. However, that is not the case. John's focus is on God, not the supporting cast of characters.

Also to be noted is the lack of any hierarchy of status or reward between believers. We will all stand as equals, all bearing a crown. There is no place in the Bible that makes it seem like some people's crowns will be better than others. In God's economy of grace, equality of reward is the payout to all believers.

The reception of a crown is a reward, one that is merited by God's grace alone. Thus, it will be our privilege to imitate the actions of the twenty-four elders and cast our crowns before God, who alone is worthy of all worship, honor, glory, and power. By throwing our crowns at the feet of Him who is worthy of all our praise, we acknowledge that all we have received is from God and is a gift of His glorious grace.

Like children who cast their coins into fountains because of the greater worth in the fountain rather than in the coins themselves, so to can we learn from the elders that value is not found in the reward given, but in the God who is the giver of good and perfect gift (Jas 1:17). There is something about the experience of God in heaven that compels believers to cast everything, including the crown of life will receive, before Him in pure, untainted adoration. I hope to someday transform trivial moments of tossing coins inside fountains into sacred ones as I convey to my children the infinite glory of God. I desire for my children to know that a day will come when we will all cast our crowns before and be "'lost in wonder, love, and praise.'"[14]

Equal Rewards

As I noted above, there will be no hierarchy of status or reward in heaven or the new creation.[15] The reward for advancing the glory

---

14 Anthony A. Hoekema, *The Bible and the Future* (Grand Rapids: Eerdmans, 1994), 287.

15 See my discussion of this in episode 18 of the *Adventures in Theology* podcast.

of God among the world is the knowledge that the glory of God is being advanced and that we are permitted to participate in such a worthy endeavor.

If I may, allow me to make this more applicable. The reward for participating in God's mission is being able to look into the eyes of others and help them go from having a hopeless destiny to one of boundless hope. The knowledge that people are redeemed and experience the endless joy of knowing God because of your obedience to God's calling to participate in their story is truly its own reward.

The reward for obedience to God's call is organically tied to the work. It is like hoisting a championship trophy alongside fellow teammates, or akin to enjoying a colorful morning in a garden during Spring after planting back in Autumn. The reward for obedience to God's calling is like these, but so much more. Now the point of all this is to highlight that the reward is tied organically to the work that Christians do. I do not believe our good deeds will earn us any different rewards from other believers; this would miss the point.

The seven letters to the churches in Rev 2–3 reveal that, despite there being a clear difference in degrees of obedience, all who end up enduring the faith will receive the same eschatological blessing.[16] What is true of the Church collectively is true of Christians individually. Again, picture a group of teammates hoisting a trophy. Do they all contribute in a similar manner on their way to securing a victory? Probably not, and that would miss the point. The glory of salvation is owed to Christ.

In a similar way, Matthew's Gospel finds Jesus recounting a parable addressing the nature of compensation for agreed upon labor (Matt 20:1–16). In this familiar parable, Jesus recites a story about a vineyard owner hiring various workers at different times of the day. Each of the workers hired agrees to the same of wages, although hired at various points throughout the day. When

---

16 The rewards listed may sound diverse, but they are saying basically the same thing. The context of the Church determines the reward; Jesus speaks to His people using words and rewards relevant to them. However, since Rev 2–3 consist of letters to the Church at large, the rewards apply to Christians from all generations.

summoned for payment at the close of the day, those hired at the start of the day realized that their pay was the same as those who started later in the day and began to protest. Nevertheless, the owner of the vineyard rebuffed their complaints and reminded them that he was free to do with his money as he saw fit. Jesus closes his parable with one of the most famous axions in the Gospels: *The last will be first and the first last* (Matt 20:16; cf. 19:30; Mark 10:31; Luke 13:30), which is a picture of eschatological leveling. Where will the first be found? Where the last are. Where will the last be found? Where the first are. The vertical social structures of our present world will be turned horizontal in God's kingdom economy.

As is clear from the parable, not all vineyard workers put in the same amount of work, and yet, at the end of the day, they all received the same pay. The point that Jesus makes in the parable is that God's gracious reward is far beyond what we deserve to be paid, regardless of the hours worked. Therefore, we have no reason to complain that someone who becomes a Christian at ninety years old will receive the same reward as the Christian who has been faithful since age nine.

On a practical note, I love the question posed by the owner of the vineyard in Matt 20:15, which literally reads: "is your eye evil because I am generous?" Such a powerful question to the hired laborers also reflects the heart of God? No matter how long we have been Christians, our God is generous with His grace. As Paul so poignantly states, our God is "able to do beyond all measure more than all we ask or think" (Eph 3:20).

The nature of parables is such that they present an underlying question. In the parable of the vineyard the question just underneath the surface is this, How does God reward us? Or said another way, What is the economy of God's reward for our work? The answer to this question is shocking to the original audience, as it no doubt is to us today. God rewards believers with radical generosity and not according to our differing accomplishments or degrees of performance. God's economy of grace grants every believer equal status and reward in His kingdom.

Commenting on this parable, Craig Blomberg avers:

> [The parable] underlines God's ultimate perspective—all true disciples are equal in his eyes. That 'the last will be first, and the first will be last' ties the parable back in with 19:30. There the 'first' were believers; the 'last,' unbelievers. Here both 'first' and 'last' are believers. The terms do not imply unequal reward but reflect the order of payment. But if all are treated equally, then all numerical positions of ranking are interchangeable, and v. 30 applies at the spiritual level too. ... There are no degrees of reward in heaven.[17]

If the motivation for doing good works is the promise of a better eternity than our fellow brothers or sisters in Christ, we misunderstand the theological nature of new creation.

Furthermore, it is important to understand that the kingdom of heaven does not operate according to human convention. In other words, our economic standards of justice and reward do not equate to God's standards of justice and reward. God rules by grace, not by merit. In the kingdom of God, where the first are last and the last first, there is no room for envious comparisons. The well-known truism has nothing to do with hierarchy or a payscale, it simply speaks to the leveling of status and reward, and how all people, in the eyes of God, stand as equals.

When we properly understand rewards in light of eschatology and kingdom equality, and in light of Matt 20:1-16, we are empowered to live out our lives as new creations, compelled by appreciation and not promotion. It is gratitude that fuels and motivates our obedience and good works.

We must stop viewing our lives as building our evangelical platform to gain rewards—fostering competition—and return to an altruistic collaboration to do what needs to be done, despite the level of acknowledgment we receive in doing the good. Plus, the one who finds the reward in the work itself ends up enjoying both even more.

Commenting on Matt 20:1-16, Daniel Doriani provides this helpful example:

---

17 Craig Blomberg, *Matthew*, NAC (Nashville: Broadman & Holman, 1992), 304.

Imagine we have three runners here in front of us. They run every day, or five times a week, and I ask the three runners, "Why do you run?" And one says, "Well, I run because when I run, I can eat anything I want, and I don't gain any weight. That's why I run." The second runner says, "I run because my father died at the age of 53, and my grandfather at the age of 51. They both had heart attacks, and I want to live a lot longer than they [did], and if I take care of my heart, I know it'll work." The third person says, "You want to know why I run? I run because when I run, my feet fly across the turf. The wind rushes through my hair. My heart beats like slow, heavy thunder in my chest. And when I run, I feel alive."

Let's ask the question: Which of these three really loves to run? The first man runs for a reward: the ability to eat any dessert he likes. The second man runs for a reward: the hope of living long. The third runner runs because he loves it. And Jesus wants us to follow Him, to obey Him because we love Him, not because we're seeking a reward. And the sad truth is that if we're thinking, "How much do I get? I've been in the kingdom longest. What do I deserve?" those who've been in the kingdom first for their whole lives will end up being last. The first will be last, and the last will be first because they delight in the grace of God.[18]

Our pursuit of the holy life is also a forsaking of our old self. We do not practice Christian holiness as a way to earn our salvation or future rewards. This pursuit is energized and empowered by the Holy Spirit and is motivated simply by our love for God and people. It is the heart of Christ being formed in us,[19] changing us from the inside out, that drives our passions and pushes us closer to what he predestined us to be. Thus, the reward becomes the good work, and the good work, the reward.

N. T. Wright helps offer this insight:

---

[18] Daniel M. Doriani, *Parables of Jesus* (NT252), Logos Mobile Education (Bellingham: Lexham Press, 2014), Unit 3, Segment 18.
[19] Cf. Gal 4:19 and Eph 4:13.

It isn't a matter of calculation, of doing a difficult job in order to be paid a wage. It is much more like working at a friendship, or a marriage, in order to enjoy the other person's company more fully. It is more like practicing golf in order that we can go out on the course and hit the ball in the right direction. It is more like learning German or Greek so that we can read some of the great poets and philosophers who wrote in those languages. The "reward" is *organically connected to the activity*, not some kind of arbitrary pat on the back, otherwise unrelated to the work that has been done. And it is always far in abundance beyond any sense of direct or equivalent payment.[20]

In a sense, those who argue for differing rewards have a point. Those who practice their faith more do receive more, but not by a merit system. It is like Wright said, those who practice golf are able to enjoy their time more on the course. We can learn from this. After all, *the joy of Jesus comes with the lifestyle of Jesus*. The peace of God comes when we walk the path of God. All these things, the real "rewards" we actually seek—are bound up with the life God wants for us. In essence, the reward of living a godly life is organically tied to the work itself. *That is why serving and loving others actually makes us feel more alive and fulfilled.* But it is never to create a hierarchy among believers—neither now nor in eternity.

Only God Is Worthy

Returning to Rev 4, we read that the elders declare to God, "You are worthy, our Lord and God" (Rev 4:11). The proclamation of God's excellency is not only true, but it is also countercultural.

In John's day, the triumphal procession of Caesar included the greeting, "You are worthy." It was common for Caesars to be considered deity, so the divine title of "Lord" was certainly used in political language, as well.

The book of Revelation is emphatically declaring that only God is worthy and only He is the true Lord and God. No political or

---

20 N. T. Wright, *Surprised by Hope* (London: SPCK, 2007), 174 (emphasis in the original).

royal figure can seize what belongs to God. After all, can anyone else claim to have "created all things?"

In the Greek text, glory, honor, and power are modified by a definite article and is rendered "the glory and the honor and the power" (Rev 4:11). The trifold use of the article classifies and categorizes the triad of praise. God does not receive part of the glory; He receives all of the glory! There is no manifestation of glory that can categorically compare to God's glory. His glory is the *par excellence* of all glory, and there is no one who gets to share in what is rightfully God's.

Sing to Yahweh a New Song

> For all the gods of the peoples are idols, but Yahweh made the heavens. Splendor and majesty are before him; strength and beauty are in his sanctuary. Ascribe to Yahweh, you families of the peoples, ascribe to Yahweh glory and strength. Ascribe to Yahweh the glory due his name; bring an offering and come into his courts. Worship Yahweh in holy array; tremble before him, all the earth. (Ps 96:5–9)

As we noted above, our praise of God's greatness does not add any worthiness to Him; it is the rightful declaration of who He is. This is the type of worship that fills the pages of Psalms. In Ps 96, the psalmist declares the praises of God in His strength and glory and encourages the reader to ascribe Him similarly.

Everything about the glory of God denotes majesty and meaning. His glory encompasses the entirety of His presence, so that where His presence is, there also is blessing. Outside of God's presence is the antithesis of blessing. Therefore, we are designed to be glory-seekers, finding meaning in God and cherishing His glory.

God is eternal, thus making Him the origin, originator, and continual sustainer of life. In the doxology in Rev 4, God is proclaimed to be the originator of life in the elders' exclamation, "You created all things" (Rev 4:11).[21] Because God is the creator of all things, this presupposes that God existed prior to what He created.

---

21 The affirmation of God's role as creator of all things is ubiquitous in the

In addition, God is the sustainer of life. The author of Hebrews concludes similarly when he affirms the Son's role in sustaining and upholding "all things by the word of [His] power" (Heb 1:3). So not only is Jesus the agent of creation (John 1:3; Col 1:16; and Heb 1:2) with God (1 Cor 8:6), He is also the sustainer of creation (Col 1:17). As Richard Bauckham correctly notes, the inclusion of Jesus within the divine work of creation highlights Jesus's uniquely divine identity.[22]

An interesting feature to point out is the conspicuous absence of Jesus from the throne room scene in Rev 4. We see God the Father ("One seated on the throne"), and we see the Holy Spirit ("seven Spirits of God"). Where is Christ during this outburst of worship? Take heart! He is just moments away from entering the scene.

Excursus: Eternal Life

The call to faith and invitation to non-believers to accept Christ and to obtain "eternal life" is one of the defining characteristics of the Christian faith. In fact, the concept of eternal life is most prevalent in the writings of John. While this phrase is not present in the book of Revelation, it is certainly manifested throughout the apocalypse in imagery like the "tree of life," "crown of life," "water of life," and "book of life."[23]

Eternal (*aiōnios*) life is both quantitative (pertaining to its duration; cf. John 6:51) and qualitative (pertaining to its condition or quality; cf. John 4:14). "It is a mode of existence referred to in Scripture characterized by either timelessness or endlessness, and especially by a qualitative difference from mortal life."[24]

---

ancient Jewish and Christian literature (cf. Gen 1:1; Isa 44:23-24; Sir 24:8; 2 Macc 1:24; 7:23; 13:14; John 1:3; Eph 3:9; and Col 1:16; Heb 1:2).

22 Richard Bauckham, *Jesus and the God of Israel: God Crucified and Other Studies on the New Testament's Christology of Divine Identity* (Grand Rapids: Eerdmans, 2009), 26-30.

23 Cf. Revelation 2:7, 10; 3:5; 13:8; 17:8; 20:12, 15; 21:6, 27; 22:1, 2, 14, 17, 19.

24 Walter A. Elwell and Barry J. Beitzel, "Eternal Life," in *Baker Encyclopedia of the Bible* (Grand Rapids: Baker Book House, 1988), 724.

We do not merely obtain immortal life—there is a Greek word for that (*aphthartos*), which we do obtain (e.g., 1 Cor 15:52). Instead, what John refers to with respect to believers is the possession of eternal life. Immortal life is very specific, focusing on the unending nature of life without decay or death. However, eternal life emphasizes "the quality of life rather than ... the unending duration of life."[25]

That said, immortal life is related to the discussion at hand. According to 1 Timothy, God "alone," possesses immortality (1 Tim 6:16). Wright correctly notes that " 'immortality' is something which only God possesses by nature, and which he then shares, as a gift of grace rather than an innate possession, with his people."[26]

It is unfair to the biblical witness to infer the inherent immortality of humanity, as this negates the symbolism of the tree of life and blinds us to the constant juxtaposition of God's way leading to life versus the antagonistic ways of rebellion leading to death or destruction.[27] In Proverbs, for example, Scripture tells us that "He who is steadfast in righteousness is to life as he who pursues evil is to death" (Prov 11:19). Now, the juxtaposition of life and death in Scripture is not limited to the literal duration of life; while including duration, the juxtaposition also denotes metaphorical usage where the results of the two divergent paths are highlighted.

The word John uses for life is *zōē*, which is a transcendent, divine sort of life. This is contrasted with the Greek word for natural life, *bios*.[28] (Of course, not every use of *zōē* deploys this meaning). John's theology of life is about the transcendent life that God possesses and shares,[29] first and foremost with His triune being, and secondarily with the beneficiaries of His grace. It is salvific in

---

25 A. Berkeley Mickelsen, "Eternal Life," edited by Chad Brand et al., *Holman Illustrated Bible Dictionary* (Nashville: Holman Bible Publishers, 2003), 511.

26 N. T. Wright, *Surprised by Hope*, 173.

27 To list a few out of the many more: Prov 13:14; 14:27; Jer 21:8; John 3:16; 5:24; Rom 6:23; 2 Tim 1:10; 1 John 3:14; Rev 2:10.

28 This is where we get the subject of "biology," which is the study of natural life.

29 William Arndt et al., *A Greek-English Lexicon of the New Testament and Other Early Christian Literature* (Chicago: University of Chicago Press, 2000), 430.

nature and implies the unending duration of eternal life plus the qualitative aspect.[30]

Zōē life can only be given by God because He is the only one who inherently possesses it. When God created us in His image, He created us with the capacity to participate in His infinite love. We are crafted with the intention to enjoy loving fellowship with the triune God, who in and of Himself has had loving community from eternity past shared by three equal but distinct persons. Bauckham puts it this way: God, out of His grace, gives to His redeemed "new life which is so united to his own eternal life that it can share his own eternity."[31] This is eternal life—knowing God intimately (John 17:3) and participating in His eternality as a gift.

We do not invite Jesus into our lives. On the contrary, He invites us into His life, which He shares with God the Father and God the Spirit in intimate fellowship. The moment our faith in Christ unites our person to His person eternal life becomes our possession as an inaugurated experience that will one day culminate in its highest potential. The experience of eternal life begins now, continues in our penultimate hope, that of heaven, and climaxes upon the arrival of our ultimate hope, a resurrected cosmos.

Eternal life is an invitation to participate in the life and love of God. God is not old; He is eternal. Life with Him will never feel old or outdated but is an ever-fresh existence in which the feeling of newness never fades. Eternal life is an "already/not yet" reality for Christians. And the best is yet to come.

This chapter concludes with these comforting words from Charles Spurgeon:

> "I give unto them eternal life," says Christ concerning his sheep. Somebody once said, "Ah, but they may lose it!" What nonsense! How can they lose eternal life? How can that be eternal which comes to an end? "Eternal life" must mean a life

---

30 Robert E. Van Voorst, "Life," edited by David Noel Freedman, Allen C. Myers, and Astrid B. Beck. *Eerdmans Dictionary of the Bible* (Grand Rapids: Eerdmans, 2000), 809.

31 Bauckham, *The Theology of the Book of Revelation*, 48–9.

that never ends; language can only be meant to conceal men's thoughts if it does not mean that. But God uses language, not for the sake of concealing the truth, but in order to reveal it; and when the Lord Jesus Christ puts everlasting life into a believer, he has everlasting life, and he will live for ever, and for this reason, he will live forever because Christ will live for ever. "Because I live, ye shall live also."[32]

---

32 C. H. Spurgeon, "Spiritual Sight and Eternal Life," in *The Metropolitan Tabernacle Pulpit Sermons*, vol. 51 (London: Passmore & Alabaster, 1905), 454.

3

The Scroll of Salvation

> *God has a definite plan for history and its consummation. It is mapped out. It is set. It will not fail.*
>
> —Daniel L. Akin[1]

Revelation 5 is inextricably connected to Rev 4.[2] Moreover, Rev 5 informs for readers on how to make sense of the judgments that will unfold in the chapters that follow. If Rev 4 is the setting of the scene, Rev 5 is the unfolding of the drama. The central focus of Rev 4 is the throne of God and creation, here in Rev 5 to focus shifts to the Lamb of God and new creation.

We begin this chapter by picking up where we left off, entranced in a vision of God's reality, namely, heaven. At this point, everything seems like another delightful day in heaven. Unending worship is taking place, and the realm of God's dwelling is unhindered by the chaos taking place on earth. However, as we begin to see, the plot of the story, that of temporal history, continues on earth. Although God is infinite and outside of time, He nevertheless is passionately concerned about the temporal progression of

---

1 Daniel L. Akin, *Exalting Jesus in Revelation*, Christ-Centered Exposition, edited by David Platt, Daniel L. Akin, and Tony Merida (Nashville: Holman Reference, 2016), 124.

2 This would be a helpful time to remind ourselves that the Bible's "chapters" and "verses" are later additions and were not present in the original text. While helpful for study, they can also be detrimental if we do not see the clear conjunctions and read the books of the Bible holistically and in light of their literary design.

his creation. And because of His concern, He has a plan for the world and is not satisfied until this plan comes to fruition.

Who Is Worthy?

> And I saw in the right hand of the one who is seated on the throne a scroll, written inside and on the back, sealed up with seven seals. And I saw a powerful angel proclaiming with a loud voice, "Who is worthy to open the scroll and to break its seals?" And no one in heaven or on earth or under the earth was able to open the scroll or to look into it. And I began to weep loudly because no one was found worthy to open the scroll or to look into it. (Rev 5:1–4)

The opening verses of Rev 5 issue a challenge to the entire universe. A mighty angel's loud voice roars across the galaxy. Consider how powerful this angel's voice must be to call out to where no one "in heaven or upon the earth or under the earth" would be worthy to respond.

The scroll that is possessed by the one seated on the throne is such that only the one who is worthy can open it. John begins to weep upon the revelation that none was found worthy. It is important that we take note of the absence of a worthy contestant. Why would the absence of a participant cause John such anguish, and what exactly is the significance of seven-seal scroll?

With respect to the scroll, it is notably no ordinary scroll. Commenting on Rev 5:1, Osborne offers the following helpful insight: "The background is Ezekiel 2:9–10, where a scroll with words of 'lament, mourning, and woe' written on both sides of it is in the hand of God and shown to Ezekiel. There and here it is a message of judgment upon those who have opposed God."[3] The scroll contains the righteous judgment of God and His plan to bring history, as we know it, to its appointed end, culminating in the birth of the new heaven and new earth (cf. Rev 21–22). What the scroll represents is the book of cosmic destiny for all of creation. It is the

---

3 Grant R. Osborne, *Revelation: Verse by Verse*, Osborne New Testament Commentaries (Bellingham: Lexham Press, 2016), 109.

plan to take back and redeem God's world and rescue God's people from the adversaries of God.

In Rev 5:4, John weeps on account of the scroll remaining sealed. In his mind, if the scroll remains sealed then evil wins.[4] John weeps vehemently at the prospect of the scroll remaining sealed. The emotion of John recorded in Rev 5:4 is points to seriousness of the scroll and, more importantly, the contents contained therein.

The scroll is held in the right hand of God, the hand of authority and power, thus requiring someone of equal stature to be able to take it from Him. It is sealed with seven seals, foreshadowing the seven judgments that would come from each seal being broken. Seven, again, is the number representing completeness, or perfection. So, here we find a scroll that is sealed with seven seals, and only someone worthy enough would be able to break its seals and reveal the contents within.

As I read the account in Rev 5:1–4, I immediately think of the famous Thor, the well-known mythical Nordic hero of Marvel Comic's fame. As readers of the comics know, Thor's hammer, Mjölner, can only be wielded by a person deemed worthy. But as worthy as Thor may have been to lift Mjölner, even he would be unworthy and unable to break the seals on the scroll. The whole universe was given the challenge, and no one could meet it. Thus, John's tears are a completely appropriate response; I imagine we would all weep loudly if present with John in the throne room of God.

It is important to note also that the final goal of new creation requires a prerequisite action. In order for the consummation of all things (cf. Eph 1:10) to occur, Christ must return and judge the world. The thought of judgment often conjures up negative connotations, however the biblical concept of judgment also exhibits positive overtones. The judgment that Christ will bring upon His return will usher in His reign, thus bringing peace to the world.

---

4 It is possible that John is alluding to Dan 12:9 and Isa 29:11, both of which refer to a sealed scroll, G. K. Beale, *The Book of Revelation: A Commentary on the Greek Text*, NIGTC (Grand Rapids: Eerdmans, 1999), 338; G. K. Beale and Sean M. McDonough, "Revelation," in *Commentary on the New Testament Use of the Old Testament* (Grand Rapids: Baker Academic, 2007), 1101.

The salvation of God is not a deliverance *away* from the physical creation, but together *with* the physical, it is an eradication of sin's destructive presence from all of creation. That is the significance of the scroll in Rev 5:1–4. It represents the beginning of the consummation of God's plan to bring salvation to its conclusion. It is the abolishment of death and the moment when Christ "hands over the kingdom to [His] God and Father (1 Cor 15:24–26).

In the previous chapter we looked at Ps 96. However, it may be fruitful to return again to Ps 96—along with Ps 97 and 98—because all three are relevant for our current discussion. Each of these Psalms in some manner personify various aspects of creation celebrating the coming judgment of God. His judgment brings deliverance from sin and evil and all that ruins humanity and creation. The judgment Jesus brings is a reversal of the wrongs that plague our existence. We cannot have a flourishing new creation without first dealing with the cancer that infects the current world order. That is why judgment is celebrated by the forces of nature. It is something to anticipate, as it will not be harmful to those who belong to God, but rather it will be our liberation! Believers should welcome the coming judgment of God because it will usher in the new creation.

However, if the scroll remains sealed then there remains no justice for the wrongs done against God and His people. And without justice administered, there remains no salvation. And without salvation, creation continues to eagerly await "the revelation of the sons of God," groaning for its ultimate redemption from decay (Rom 8:19–22).

Behold the Lamb

> And one of the elders said to me, "Do not weep! Behold, the lion of the tribe of Judah, the root of David, has conquered, so that he can open the scroll and its seven seals." And I saw in the midst of the throne and of the four living creatures and in the midst of the elders a Lamb standing as though slaughtered, having seven horns and seven eyes, which are the seven spirits

of God sent into all the earth. And he came and took the scroll from the right hand of the one who was seated on the throne. (Rev 5:5–7)

Every Sunday, it is common to find children drawing pictures of larger-than-life biblical characters in Sunday school classes across the world. Such pictures depict events like Noah's ark, Moses parting the Red Sea, or Jesus walking on water. However, you may be hard-pressed to find hanging on refrigerators a portrait of Jesus as a "Lamb standing as though slaughtered, having seven horns and seven eyes, which are the seven spirits of God sent into all the earth" (Rev 5:6). Not only would such a depiction be unnerving for those who catch a glimpse as they open the fridge, but it would only be the representation of a young child's wild imagination. No doubt John's description of Jesus as a slain lamb only scratched the surface of what his eyes had truly witnessed. But how could this be so?

The answer to this is found in the genre of Revelation. It is important to remember that not everything recorded in apocalyptic literature is meant to be one harmonious picture. While the words come together and make since when you add up the meaning, however, this is not the case when one tries to cohere the symbols *before* rendering the meaning of the symbols.

Nonetheless, one simply cannot adequately portray Jesus any better than what we read in Rev 5. He is both a lion and a lamb; both standing and slaughtered; adorned with seven horns and eyes, which are the seven spirits of God. What we find here in John's vision is far more horrifying than it is encouraging!

A further feature that jumps from the pages of Revelation is the author's penchant for metaphors. A metaphor is the substitution of a literal meaning for a different sense in order to provide a comparison between the two. Some of the more common examples of biblical metaphors are found in Ps 23:1 ("Yahweh is my shepherd; I will not lack for anything"); John 6:35 ("Jesus said to them, 'I am the bread of life'"); 8:12 ("Then Jesus spoke to them again, saying, 'I am the light of the world'"); just to name a few. The purpose of metaphorical language is to provide a reader with a vivid word picture that heightens the comparison between two concepts or ideas.

However, to complicate things a bit more, what we discover in Revelation 5 is the mixing of metaphors. Briefly, to mix metaphors is provide a reader with rather confusing or incongruent comparison. For example, in John 10 Jesus tells his disciples that he is both the *door* and *the good shepherd*. On the surface, one cannot make a corresponding connection between the door that the sheep go in and out of and the shepherd who guides and protects the sheep.

In Rev 5:5–7, we find such mixing of metaphors. The first is found in response to John's weeping: "Do not weep! Behold, the *lion of the tribe of Judah*, the *root of David*, has conquered, so that he can open the scroll and its seven seals" (5:5). Here, one of the elders refers to Jesus as both a lion *and* a root, both of which are messianic references from the Old Testament (lion: Gen 49:9; root: Isa 11:1, 10; cf. Rev 22:16).

As noted above, both titles—lion and root—are messianic and originate in the Old Testament. The lion, an invariable symbol of strength and royalty, is applied to Jesus as the messianic conqueror. It is also possible that the lion imagery highlights the lion-like characteristics found in Prov 28:1b, where the author posits that "the righteous are bold like a lion."

The botanical imagery of a root appears again in Rev 22:16, where Jesus declares Himself to be the "root and descendant of David." As the promised descendant of David (2 Sam 7:12–16; 1 Chr 17:11–14; Ps 89; cf. Matt 1:1), the Messiah was promised to sit on the throne of David and rule forever.

Be that as it may, the description of Jesus as the root of David is a peculiar one. In what way can Jesus be both the root *and* descendant of David? On the one hand, Jesus is the originator of David. It is He who created all things, including the person of David. But on the other hand, as one born of a woman (Gal 4:4), Christ shares in the lineage of David through both his mother (Matt 1:2–17) and father (Luke 3:23–38).

Theologically speaking, the answer to the question of how Jesus can be both David's creator and his descendant is found in what theologians have termed the *hypostatic union*. What this term essentially means is that Jesus, in His incarnation, is both fully God *and* fully human.[5] It is in light of this union that Jesus is able to function as both creator of all and a genuine human, all in the person of the God-man, Jesus Christ.

In Rev 5:6 we again find a mixing of metaphors, when Jesus is described as "a Lamb *standing* as though *slaughtered*." It is rather obvious that a slaughtered lamb does not stand after being offered as a sacrifice. However, this is exactly how John envisions Jesus, as that of a conquering sacrificial lamb. Beale rightly concludes that "Christ's death, the end-time sacrifice of the messianic Lamb, [is] interpreted as a sacrifice that not only redeems but also conquers."[6]

This mixing of metaphors could be considered a literary blunder by modern constraints, but with respect to the genre of apocalyptic, such occurrences are both common and acceptable. Each metaphor has imagery that communicates something about the subject, but when read together it would come across as though contradictory. It is imperative that we understand what John is communicating about the Lamb and how it informs the christology of Revelation.

Amid John's vision and subsequent lament, one of the elders instructs to cease his weeping, proclaiming that lion of Judah has conquered and is thus able to open the scroll. This victory has *already* been secured, which is communicated by the aorist tense of the Greek verb *enikēsen*.[7] The Lamb "has conquered," or "has prevailed." It is not an awaited event, but a past action that provides the foundation for the Christian's confidence. It has already

---

5 "[T]he hypostatic union consists in the fact that the Son of God is the subject of everything that the Bible maintains about Christ, both the affirmations about the divine, and those concerning the human. Speaking with more precision, the theological statement 'hypostatic union' expresses the concept for which the second hypostasis of the Trinity was united to a perfect and concrete human nature in such a way as to constitute through it the principle of incommunicable subsistence and to be the subject of its natural and individual properties," Basil Studer, "Hypostatic Union," in *Encyclopedia of Ancient Christianity*, ed. Angelo Di Berardino (Downers Grove: IVP Academic, 2014), 309–10.

6 Beale, *Revelation*, 351.

7 When the aorist tense is deployed in the indicative mood, it communicates the verbal action having been accomplished in past time (with respect to the writer). The indicative mood is the only mood that communicates time within the aspect of the verbal tense.

happened! And so, the gospel according to Revelation begins to unravel before John's very eyes.

It would be safe to assume that John's vision of a lion and a slaughtered lamb left him in utter words shock. It is not that John was unaware of Christ being the paschal lamb (cf. John 1:29). The question is, why would the elder tell John to look for a lion when what he saw before him was a lamb? The irony is found in the drastic contrast between the two. However, the metaphorical description we are given about Jesus is that He is both lion and a lamb.

A Final Sacrifice

A striking feature of Rev 5:6 is the sacrificial imagery utilized by John to describe Jesus. He is referred to in rather graphic terms as a slaughtered lamb (Rev 5:6; cf. 5:12; 7:14; 12:12; 13:8). The background for John's sacrificial lamb imagery is found in two primary Old Testament accounts: Passover (Exod 12:1–28; cf. Deut 16:1–8) and Isaiah's Suffering Servant (Isa 52:13–53:12).

In the Passover account in Exod 12, the Israel is ordered to take for themselves a young lamb for an offering. They are to slaughter the lamb on the fourteenth day of the month and place the blood from the sacrifice on the frames of the door. It is the blood of the slaughtered lamb, the *paschal lamb*, that saves the firstborn of Israel from death.

In the New Testament, the paschal lamb motif is taken up by Jesus. At the outset of Jesus's ministry, John the Baptist declares Jesus to be "[t]he Lamb of God who takes away the sin of the world!" (John 1:29). Likewise, in his first letter to the Corinthian church Paul utilizes Passover imagery to remind his readers that "Christ, our Passover lamb, has been sacrificed" (1 Cor 5:7b ESV).

The Suffering Servant of Isa 53 is perhaps the most vivid Old Testament picture of the Messiah's suffering death for his people. He is described as having "no form or majesty ... and no appearance" to "take pleasure in" (53:2b); "He was despised and rejected ... a man of suffering, and acquainted with sickness ... one from whom other hid their faces" (53:3). In no way was Servant respected or look upon as someone worthy of honor. He was a man so despised by his people that they could not bear to even look at him.

However, in a plot twist of for the ages, it is this Servant that God has chosen to be the very one to bear the sins of the people. Not only did he lift up the sickness and carry away the pain of the people, but more importantly, "he was pierced for [their] transgressions and crushed for [their] iniquities," and it was "by his wounds that [they] we healed" (53:5). The Servant was "brought like a lamb to the slaughter" (53:7b), where "Yahweh let fall on him the iniquity" of all people (53:6b). This Suffering Servant was the sacrificial lamb "who bore the sin of many" (53:12c).

Thus, in Rev 5 Christ appears before John as the slaughtered lamb who stands in the place of sinners. He stands not merely as the paschal lamb, doomed to die, nor as the Suffering Servant who bore the sins of many, but as the resurrected Christ.

Two words of importance in Rev 5:6 are "standing" and "slaughtered." In the Greek text of Rev 5:6, these two verbs are in the perfect tense. The perfect tense of a verb often communicates a completed action in the *past* with continual results and ramifications in the *present*. Regarding the John's use of the verb "slaughter," Akin posits that "[t]here is permanence about the scars of His sacrifice. There is also a once-and-for-all nature with abiding results to His sacrifice."[8] Leon Morris agrees with Akin, noting that "[t]he Greek perfect tense ... signifies that the Lamb was not only slain at a point of time, but that the efficacy of his death is still present in all its power."[9] Therefore, the stative aspect of the perfect tense helps color the powerful results that have come into existence due to the purposeful death of Christ. His atoning death is essential to biblical doctrine, so much so that only the perfect can adequately convey the nuance of Christ's graphic death.

Christ will always be known as the slaughtered Lamb, and He will always bear the wounds that mark his body. It will be a token

---

8 Akin, *Exalting Jesus in Revelation*, 126. See also Beale, *Revelation*, 351–352. "John deploys the perfect participle *esphagmenon* ('having been slain') to express an abiding condition as a result of the past act of being slain."

9 Leon Morris, *Revelation: An Introduction and Commentary*, TNTC 20 (Downers Grove: InterVarsity Press, 1987), 98.

of His love for us and the sacrifice by which He rescued us. As Charles Spurgeon so poetically avers:

"There is one mark in that hand which has made it specially dear to you, for 'the hand of the Lord' from which you receive everything is a nail-pierced hand, for it is the hand of the man Christ Jesus as well as the hand of the almighty God; and hard by the print of the nail is your own name, for he has said to you, 'I have graven thee upon the palms of my hands.'"[10]

As is the case above, the Greek text conveys the action of Christ standing with the perfect tense verb. The idea here is that Christ's standing is a reference to His resurrection and recalls Rev 1:18, where Jesus proclaims, "I was dead, and behold I am alive forever and ever." Neither death nor the grave could not contain the Lord of glory (Acts 2:24).

We must not ignore the location of Christ's standing: "in the midst of the throne." He stands not with the rest of the creation; Christ is standing He is at the center (cf. Rev 7:17). This helps to explains why the redeemed stand simultaneously in front of the throne and in front of the Lamb (Rev 7:9). Christ is standing beside the Father, who is on the throne. This makes sense considering the later reference to the "throne of God and of the Lamb" (Rev 22:3; cf. 22:1).

While there is only one throne, there are two occupants. Likewise, God and the Lamb together form the temple of the new Jerusalem (Rev 21:22). It is possible that John's trinitarian theology is on display, before the term "trinitarian" formally came into usage. The single throne of God has the first two persons of the Godhead (Father and Son) occupying the throne simultaneously.

John describes the Lamb as having "seven horns," which are a symbol of perfect strength and kingly might. By using the number seven, the apocalyptic imagery suggests that the Lamb is omnipotent and all-powerful. Furthermore, His "seven eyes" denote His omniscience. His omniscience is also demonstrated through the "seven Spirits of God who have been sent into all the earth" (cf. Zech 4:10). By referring to the Spirit being "sent out into all the

---

10 C. H. Spurgeon, "God's Hand at Eventide," in *The Metropolitan Tabernacle Pulpit Sermons*, vol. 58 (London: Passmore & Alabaster, 1912), 88.

earth," John may be alluding to the Day of Pentecost, "when the Spirit came upon the disciples and empowered them to take the gospel to the whole world" (cf. Acts 1:8; 2:33).[11]

What we as readers must take from the account in Rev 5:5-7 is the worthiness of the lamb to open the scroll (Rev 5:7). The lamb is heaven's answer to earth's dire need, a king who has come to conqueror creation's catastrophic disease. And by conquering over all evil, He has rid our hearts of sin. Now, He will open the scroll and rid the world of the curse. Eschatology, therefore, is birthed in a proper understanding of the person and work of Christ. Only when we understand who Christ is and what he has accomplished can we rightfully speak of the benefits believers gain as a result of the work of Christ in the eschaton.

God Will Set All Things Right

In all honesty, everyone wants justice. When we were kids, we wanted our siblings to get caught doing something wrong. When someone cuts us off on the freeway and speeds past us, we want them to get a speeding ticket. Not only do we want that, but we also want the satisfaction of watching the police car turn on their lights to pull them over. However, not all examples of justice are the same, nor are they really matters of justice at all.

True justice is just that, it is *just*. Consider a businessman who underpays his employees and hoards the money for himself. Think about the leader of a terrorist organization who sneaks away into the shadows uncaught. There are times when it is perfectly valid—and *right*—to seek justice.[12] And these examples allow a just society to administer legal, civil, and even sometimes militaristic justice.

However, when it comes to the biblical drama it may appear that evil is reigning triumphant. When one looks out at the world, it is easy to lose heart. Has God has grown calloused to all the suffering in the world caused by evil? Has He forgotten His creation

---

11 Paul Gardner, *Revelation: The Compassion and Protection of Christ*, Focus on the Bible Commentary (UK: Christian Focus Publications, 2002), 84.

12 Interestingly, the Greek word *dikaiosynē* can be glossed as either "justice" or "righteousness," which should tell us something about how these two concepts are closely related and explain one another.

and left it to suffer all sorts of maladies? Not at all! In fact, no one is more adamant about eradicating evil than God. And He has a plan to eliminate all evil and reverse the curse that was set upon His creation.

In fact, God's redemptive plan and the end of evil this is not unique to the book of Revelation. "The motif of God's coming reign defeating evil and establishing righteousness [is] a central theme in apocalyptic literature such as the book of Daniel," J. Richard Middleton writes. In fact, Daniel "envisions the establishment of god's universal and everlasting kingdom, as a dominion is taken from the unjust rulers of this world and given to God's holy people ([Dan] 7:13–14, 27)."[13]

When it comes to justice, make no mistake: God will administer it with enduring and irreversible results. God's enactment of His justice may be *delayed* for a time, but it is certainly not *denied*. We can rest assured that God will set all things right. And when He bangs the gavel of His righteous judgment, the entire world will feel the weight of it.

Yet, whatever qualms we have with biblical ideas of justice and judgment we must remember who the coming judge is. Yes, Jesus is the coming judge—but remember who He was and is. Remember His character as showcased in the Gospels. We can trust this judge to act with mercy and justice. We can trust the lion-lamb to have the discerning ability to know when to be as fierce as a lion and as gentle as a lamb. I like how Wright puts it:

> God is the living and loving creator, who must either judge the world or stand accused of injustice, of letting wickedness triumph. People who have lived in societies where evil flourishes unchecked will tell you that it is a nightmare. To live in a world where that was the case for ever would be hell.[14]

---

13 J. Richard Middleton, *A New Heaven and a New Earth: Reclaiming Biblical Eschatology* (Grand Rapids: Baker Academic, 2014), 244. Middleton goes on to show how "the coming of God's reign in history to rectify a world out of whack with his original intent ... had, by the time of Jesus, become a central expectation in much Jewish life" (245).

14 N. T. Wright, *Paul for Everyone: Galatians and Thessalonians* (London: Society for Promoting Christian Knowledge, 2004), 143.

In this interim period, therefore, we are to be conduits of God's mercy as we lead others to the same mercy that we ourselves have experienced. It is our duty to give mercy even when it is not merited. We are to forgive the unforgivable that we see in others, because God has forgiven the unforgivable in us.

This is the part of history in which mercy is extended through the nail-pierced hands of Jesus. This is our chance to receive such divine forgiveness, as Heb 9:28 indicates in referring to judgment: "so also the Messiah, having been offered once to bear the sins of many, will appear a second time, not to bear sin, but to bring salvation to those who are eagerly waiting for Him." Although we are not through with the throne room vision just yet (Rev 4–5), hopefully what we are beginning to understand more fully the penultimate verse of Scripture: "Come, Lord Jesus" (Rev 22:20).

4

The Coronation of Heaven's King

> *My desire is that my Lord would give me broader and deeper thoughts, to feed myself with wondering at His love.*
> —Samuel Rutherford[1]

As believers, we rejoice at the ascension of the resurrected Christ. Jesus in his resurrected state physically and material ascended into heaven where he now intercedes for his people (Heb 7:25; 9:24; cf. Rom 8:34). In truth, the reality of Christ's resurrection forces us to accept that heaven is far more material than we think.

Although Christ's resurrection was a bodily event, this does not imply His physicality is the same as ours. This can be seen in Paul's discussion about the nature of the resurrection body in 1 Cor 15:35–49. In 1 Cor 15:50, Paul states in no uncertain terms that "flesh and blood is not able to inherit the kingdom of God." So, for Paul the resurrected body, while truly human, is in some sense altogether different than the flesh and blood bodies that humans possess this side of glory.

That said, it is important that we reconcile the idea that the different dimensions of heaven—God's dwelling, and earth, our abode—are closer than we think. And not only are they close in proximity, but they are close in rule as well. The one who rules

---

1 Samuel Rutherford, *Letters of Samuel Rutherford*, edited by Andrew A. Bonar (Edinburgh and London: Oliphant Anderson and Ferrier, 1891), 257.

heaven also rules earth. Or, to put it another way, the Lord of heaven is also the Lord of the entire cosmos.

When thinking about the ascension, we also cannot help but wonder what happened to Jesus after His entrance into heaven.[2] The author of Hebrews does shed some light on this question. For example, we note that in Heb 1 that when Jesus entered heaven the angels worshipped Him (Heb 1:6). Another element of Jesus ascension into heaven is that of intercession. As our perpetual high priest, Jesus "lives in order to intercede on [our] behalf" (Heb 7:25). Jesus "did not enter into a sanctuary made by hands, a mere copy of the true one, but into heaven itself, now to appear in the presence of God *on our behalf*" (Heb 9:24, emphasis added). While do not know exactly all that Jesus did upon his entry into heaven, we nevertheless do know that he was busy ministering on behalf of his people.

The Royalty of Jesus

In Rev 1:5, Jesus refers to Himself as the "firstborn from the dead." The title "firstborn" occurs in a number of places in the New Testament. In Rom 8:29, Jesus is "the firstborn among many brothers." In Colossians, He is "the firstborn over all creation" (Col 1:15) and "the firstborn from the dead" (Col 1:18). And, in Heb 1:6, it is God who "brings the firstborn into the world."

With respect to the passages found in Colossians, the title of "firstborn" plays a significant part in our understanding of christology. The honorific title is best understood considering the immediate context of Col 1, specifically Paul's use of the familial "Son" (Col 1:13–14), a designation found often in John's Gospel. Such titles as firstborn and Son of God carry a certain significance when applied to humans, which helps to uncover the even richer meaning when we are speaking of the unique divine Messiah.[3]

As the Son of God, Jesus functions as the mediator between those who are in union with Him (those who are "in Christ") and

---

[2] Cf. Luke 24:51–52; Acts 1:1–11.

[3] Jarl Fossum, "Son of God," edited by David Noel Freedman, *The Anchor Yale Bible Dictionary* (New York: Doubleday, 1992), 133.

the heavenly Father. His royal privilege was foreshadowed in the Old Testament. For instance, in Ps 89:27 the psalmist writes, "I will also make him the firstborn, the highest of the kings of the earth." As noted above, Jesus is the firstborn, the one who arrives as the substance of what was always a shadow prior to His incarnation. Moses was a type of covenant mediator. David was a type of king. But both were penultimate, not *the* ultimate. Thus, Jesus serves as the eschatological fulfillment of the Old Testament types and shadows.

When we speak of Jesus as the firstborn, we are referring to a position of privilege and preeminence. In Ps 89:27[4] the same Greek term for "firstborn" is used. What is clear from the context is that the psalmist is not referring to physical birth. In Col 1, Paul could have used a few different Greek words to communicate that Jesus was created or formed before the rest of creation, but this was not the case. Rather, firstborn is a clear title of royal supremacy acting as the ambassador of divine presence.

Psalm 2 reaffirms this concept and establishes a predominant connection between the functional title Son of God and royal Messianic power:

> The point which appears to unite those two quotations [speaking of the connection between Psalm 2:7 and Isaiah 40:1] is the kingly power associated with the title "Son of God" in the OT. While royal power is implied in the verse from Isaiah, where God's "chosen servant" (Isa 42:1) will establish "justice in the earth" (Isa 42:3b–4a) ... Originally an enthronement psalm, Psalm 2 was composed to celebrate the assumption of royal power by a king chosen by God to rule his chosen people ... Verse 6 declares the enthronement; *v 7 declares the enthroned king to be God's son*, thus establishing the link between royal power and the title "Son of God" in the Psalm. ... "Son of God" will be a title for each succeeding king of Israel of the Davidic line.[5]

---

4 Psalm 88:28 in the Septuagint, the Greek translation of the Old Testament.
5 Paul J. Achtemeier, "Mark, Gospel of," edited by David Noel Freedman, *The Anchor Yale Bible Dictionary* (New York: Doubleday, 1992), 551–2. Italics mine.

Christ's life, death, and resurrection all serve to illustrate the messiahship of Jesus and His kingship and redemption of God's people. The New Testament's language and use of titles like "Son of God" and "firstborn" are meant to be read in light of the eschatology of the Old Testament. What we can conclude about those titles is that Jesus is the antitype, while all before Him were imperfect. The only true Messiah who could be everything humanity needed Him to be was an incarnation of Yahweh, Israel's God. Therefore, the condescension of the incarnation demands the Lord ascend to His rightful place.

At Jesus's ascension into heaven and his session at the right hand of God,[6] the idea came to fruition that God's universal reign has been inaugurated in and through the person and work of *the* true "Son of God."[7] Colossians 1:15b reaffirms this, declaring that Jesus, as the firstborn, is preeminent over the scope "of all creation." The Greek word *pas*, "all," is in the singular and illustrates how *every* part of the whole is touched. In this case, the meaning is clear: There is not a single square inch of the universe that Jesus's preeminent Lordship does not cover.

To summarize, calling Jesus the "firstborn of all creation" is best understood in the sense that Jesus is the prince who will inherit everything. The eternal sonship of Jesus does not contradict His eternal deity;[8] it simply highlights a coming into kingly authority that was always destined to be His.

The Coronation

Before moving on to Rev 5, there is one final to consider. Daniel 7 has perhaps the closest parallels to the book of Revelation,

---

6 Cf. Acts 2:33–36; 7:55–56; Rom 8:34; Eph 1:20; Col 3:1; Hebrews 1:3, 13; 8:1; 10:12–13; 12:2; 1 Pet 3:21b–22; Rev 3:21.

7 Cf. David G. Peterson, *The Acts of the Apostles*, PNTC (Grand Rapids: Eerdmans, 2009), 431.

8 Fred Sanders published a web article that helps to understand how Jesus can be the eternal Son of God without any question to His deity. Sanders argues that the Christian tradition makes it clear that "Christ's sonship goes all the way back into the being of God." See: "Forever and Always the Son: Why We Treasure Eternal Generation," *Desiring God*, last modified March 16, 2020, https://www.desiringgod.org/articles/forever-and-always-the-son.

a parallel that is most likely influenced by the apocalyptic genre found in both writings. In Dan 7:1–8 the author records a vision in which four beats arise on the scene, representing various nations coming to power. In verses 9–12, the four beasts are brought before the judgment seat of God (who is called the "Ancient of Days" in this passage). One beast is immediately destroyed, with the remaining three permitted to rule a little longer, while remaining under the sovereign eye of God.

Then we come to verses 13 and 14.

In Dan 7:13–14, the Ancient of Days will judge those who oppose Him and ultimately bring all people under subjection of the special figure who is like the "Ancient of Days" but also distinct from Him:

> I continued watching in the night visions, and suddenly one like a son of man was coming with the clouds of heaven. He approached the Ancient of Days and was escorted before him. He was given dominion, and glory, and a kingdom; so that those of every people, nation, and language should serve him. His dominion is an everlasting dominion that will not pass away, and his kingdom is one that will not be destroyed. (Dan 7:13–14)

Daniel 7 is nothing less than a coronation ceremony, whereby the Ancient of Days crowns this mysterious figure who is "like a son of man."[9] By a coronation ceremony, we mean that we are watching one who was anointed to be king receive the crown and status that he was appointed for! This "son of man" figure is about to inherit a kingdom that will be "everlasting" and "will not pass away." A strange ability of this figure is that he "was coming with the clouds"; in essence, he was *riding* the clouds. In the ancient world, it was believed that only a deity could ride the clouds.[10]

---

9 "This scene is a coronation, as becomes evident in verse 14; recalling in different language the words of Psalm 2:6: 'I have installed my king on Zion, my holy hill.'" Bob Fyall, *Daniel: A Tale of Two Cities*, Focus on the Bible Commentary (UK: Christian Focus Publications, 1998), 105; Cf. also, Stephen R. Miller. *Daniel*, vol. 18, NAC (Nashville: Broadman & Holman, 1994), 207.

10 "In Israelite theology, Yahweh is the high God and also is portrayed as

The description of this "son of man" closely parallels Jesus's description of Himself (Matt 24:30; 26:64; cf. Acts 1:11). "Son of Man" was Jesus's most frequent self-designation (occurring 82 times in the Gospels). This not only catches our attention, it also requires an explanation. The only passage in the Old Testament that has the explanatory power for such self-designated emphasis is in fact Dan 7.

The most compelling evidence for the messianic identification of the son of man is furnished by Christ himself. In Mark 14:61–62 he identified himself as that "Son of Man sitting at the right hand of the Mighty One and coming on the clouds of heaven." There is no other passage in the Old Testament to which Christ could have been referring. Furthermore, when Christ made the claim, the high priest said, "You have heard the blasphemy" (Mark 14:64), demonstrating that Jesus was understood to ascribe deity to himself. Young asserts, "The employment of this title by Jesus Christ is one of the strongest evidences that He attributed Deity to Himself."[11]

When on trial, Jesus unambiguously reveals His identity. Caiaphas asks, and Jesus responds by attributing the "son of man" identity to Himself. Caiaphas understood that Jesus was claiming to be the cloud-riding figure of Dan 7:13 who was equal to Yahweh—and that was an intolerable blasphemy.[12] The book of Revelation, likewise, presents Jesus as the one coming with clouds of heaven (Rev 1:7; 14:14–15), harkening back to the "son of man" figure in Dan 7. It is important that we not miss this, for this background functions as the foundation of Rev 5. What we read in Rev 5 must not forgo the denotations of what the scene is conveying, namely the coronation of heaven's king.

Therefore, Dan 7:13–14 highlights the prophetic scene of the coronation of Christ foreshadowed in Old Testament apocalyptic

---

the rider on the clouds." Victor Harold Matthews, Mark W. Chavalas, and John H. Walton, *The IVP Bible Background Commentary: Old Testament*, (Downers Grove: InterVarsity Press, 2000), Daniel 7:13–14.

11 Miller, *Daniel*, 209. The parallel passage to Mark 14:62 (which is a stacked citation of Ps 110:1 and Dan 7:13) is Matt 26:64.

12 Michael S. Heiser, *The Unseen Realm: Recovering the Supernatural Worldview of the Bible* (Bellingham: Lexham Press, 2015), 253.

imagery. The Messianic cloud rider is being crowned as the king over all of creation, destined to rule with the Ancient of Days. The Messianic Lord, who now sits at the right hand of the Father, rules from heaven and oversees the events imprinted in the scroll of salvation.

Jesus the Prince

In the ancient world kings were warriors. In fact, across the ancient Near East you find traditions of how each culture had a particular ritual in which the soon-to-be-king would showcase their "worthiness" to be coronated as king by performing heroic feats. In Assyria, for example, they conducted a royal hunt, where the prince would kill a lion to prove himself worthy of kingship.

In the New Testament, Jesus is depicted as the true warrior-king. He did not take the crown without first proving that He was worthy of it, namely by liberating His subjects from the captivity to sin and the powers of darkness. Only after confronting evil in His ministry, absorbing sin on the cross, and overcoming the power of the grave did He ascend into heaven where He was to coronated as the eternal king.

Part of the reason Jesus is revealed to us as God's "Son" is because He is the Prince who rises to a royal reign within the chronology of redemptive history. Revelation 4 depicts God the Father sitting on the throne. I would suggest that Rev 5, then, presents a remarkable vision of the incarnate Son's ascension to the throne and coronation as the "King of kings" (cf. Rev 17:14; 19:16). The events that take place are all part of the Son of God's coronation ceremony, after which He will rule heaven *and* earth alongside God the Father.

The Gospels show us how the Lord, Yahweh Himself, inserted Himself into human history by becoming a man to redeem sinful people, and afterwards became King of His own creation through His ascension and coronation. [13] And while He was worthy of the

---

13 Cf. "When Jesus speaks of 'the son of man coming on the clouds', he is not talking about the second coming, but, in line with the Daniel 7 text he is quoting, about his vindication after suffering. The 'coming' is an upward, not a downward, movement." N. T. Wright, *Surprised by Hope* (London: SPCK, 2007), 137–8.

praise He received at His coronation, His humility and sacrifice solidified His worthiness before all creation. The narrative of the Bible truly is the most phenomenal story; no person could have conceived of it. The Bible remains an unfathomable depth of wisdom, "inspired by God and profitable for teaching, for reproof, for correction, [and] for training in righteousness" (2 Tim 3:16).

A New Song

> And when he took the scroll, the four living creatures and the twenty-four elders fell down before the Lamb, each one of whom had a harp and golden bowls full of incense, which are the prayers of the saints. And they were singing a new song, saying, "You are worthy to take the scroll and to open its seals, because you were slaughtered, and bought people for God by your blood from every tribe and language and people and nation, and made them a kingdom and priests to our God, and they will reign on the earth." And I looked, and I heard the voice of many angels around the throne and of the living creatures and of the elders, and their number was ten thousand times ten thousand and thousands times thousands, saying with a loud voice, "Worthy is the Lamb who was slaughtered to receive power and riches and wisdom and strength and honor and glory and praise!" (Rev 5:8–12)

The coronated king has inaugurated the long-awaited New Covenant, which naturally initiates the singing of a new song in heaven. Grant Osborne sheds light on the Old Testament background on new songs:

> New songs are frequent in the Psalms, expressing a new worship inspired by the mercies of God (Pss 33:3; 40:3; 96:1; 98:1; 144:9; 149:1). In Isaiah 42:10 the new song is eschatological, looking ahead to the appearance of the Servant of Yahweh and "new things." There is a new kind of song to celebrate the coming of the new age that is soon to appear.[14]

---

14 Grant R. Osborne, *Revelation: Verse by Verse*, Osborne New Testament

Earlier in Rev 4:8, a song was sung to God by the four living creatures, where "day and night never cease" to sing. Now in Rev 5:8–10 the four living creatures transition their worship in order to sing a "new song" to the Lamb. What could possibly be a higher expression and identification of deity than to have the heavenly angels transition their unending song, dedicated to celebrating the holiness of God, over to the worship of Jesus? Nothing or no one is able to stop the unceasing song of worship to God except one who is ontologically equal, and according to John that equal is the Lamb who was slain. The moment the Lamb takes the scroll from God He becomes corecipient with God of the entirety of heaven's praise.

The song of Rev 4:8 was sung by the old creation, the four living creatures; however, the new song of Rev 5:9–10 is the song of the redeemed new creation. The twenty-four elders cry out: "You are worthy, our Lord and God, to receive glory and honor and power, for you created all things, and by your will they were created and have their being" (Rev 4:11). And when the angel asks, "Who is worthy to break the seals and open the scroll?" (5:2), John laments that "no one was found who was worthy to open the scroll or look inside" (5:4), but with the appearance of the Lion-Lamb appears it becomes clear that He alone is worthy to be entrusted by God with the execution of His plans of salvation and of kingship (5:9, 12),[15] thus summing up the prophetic aspirations and aims of the promised and long-awaited Messianic King.[16]

The definite victory of the Messiah calls for a new song, because now the dawn of the new creation has been inaugurated and the purchase has been paid for in full. This is even more spectacular than God's original creation of the world.

The One Who Is Worthy

Finally, in Rev 5:9, we find the answer to the question first posed

---

Commentaries (Bellingham: Lexham Press, 2016), 114–15.

15 Moisés Silva, ed., *New International Dictionary of New Testament Theology and Exegesis* (Grand Rapids: Zondervan, 2014), 341.

16 I prefer the title Christ (*christos* in Greek) to be dynamically rendered as "Messianic King," to bring out the combined Jewish and kingly overtones to the role.

by the mighty angel in verse 5:2. "Who is worthy?" is answered by the worship and praise of the Lamb. This is not merely an ethical worthiness, although ethical worthiness is undoubtedly necessary. Rather, this is an inherent worth, a sort of sufficiency to stand in equal authority with God to carry out the plan of redemptive salvation. The worthiness of the Lamb is credited not solely to His person, but more emphatically to His work—namely through His death and resurrection. Similar to the worship of the one on the throne in Rev 4, the doxology of the Lamb focuses on His redemptive actions. What He has accomplished by ransoming people and making them royal priests to God solidified his worthiness of the title of Messiah.

The chorus of heaven shouts the accolades of Christ's atoning sacrifice, culminating in Jesus being our greater and permanent Passover Lamb.[17] The royal Son of God had a mission to accomplish, a conquest to champion before the scroll was to be opened. His ascribed worthiness is nothing short of the finished work of His prophetic life—His conquering death, life-giving resurrection, and glorious ascension.

The Messianic methods of salvation are just as astounding as the mission itself. The original audience of Revelation would have seen the natural comparison between the self-glorifying rule of Caesar and the self-sacrifice of the Lamb. The Lion of Judah secured the victory through sacrificing Himself as the paschal Lamb. Christ's way of conquering is countercultural no matter the era the reader comes from, whether it be the first century or the twenty-first. I believe the reason He kept the nail-scarred hands (even after His resurrection) was to be a token of His love for those who trust Him.

The Lamb is worthy because his power is antithetical to that of Caesar. He exerts a power not to destroy or to oppress, but a power that is manifested by his love and in His willingness to give all of himself for the sake of those who belong to Him. It is in His willingness to die for His own where liberation is found.[18] As Scrip-

---

17 As we have already said of 1 Cor 5:7. Cf. also Heb 10:12.
18 Allan A. Boesak, *Comfort and Protest: Reflections on the Apocalypse of John of Patmos* (Philadelphia: Westminster, 1987), 56–7.

ture says, "by His wounds we are healed."[19] Our adoration of Jesus's self-sacrifice for the benefit of others motivates us to sacrifice ourselves for others at the drastic expense of our very own lives.[20]

The victory of God in and through the Messianic Lamb is decisive and complete. This is the meaning of Jesus's wondrous words from the cross as He cried out, "It is finished" (John 19:30). This powerful proclamation is one Greek word, *tetelestai*. Here we find another example of how the original language helps paint the dramatic effect of Jesus's sacrifice with another poignant example of the perfect tense.

In essence, it is said of Jesus: "All that is needed to pay for salvation has been paid in full; the transaction is complete." Not just any sacrifice would suffice, for our debt was far too great and our condition far too lethal to pay and reverse ourselves. Thus, the infinite had to become like the finite creation, and through the blood of God we have learned the weight of our sin and the love of our Savior.

The slaughtered Lamb forces us to contemplate both the righteousness and the love of God. The Son of God who knew no sin also never knew a moment of separation from His Father until He tasted the separation we deserve. Because of what Jesus has done, we can cherish and anticipate the words that come from God: "Everything is accomplished" (Rev 21:6a).

These words come following the judgment of God and the final judgment of all evil. The transaction has happened; the purchase was paid in full for our salvation. Now we await the full ramifications of the transaction, as God will judge the old creation and usher in the new creation, ultimately bringing substance to the words "Everything is accomplished."

We notice that the worship given to the Lamb in Rev 5 is ascribed to His activity. When we celebrate the actions of God, we affirm the identity of God. For example, it is one thing to say, "God is good." This is, of course, true. But it is another thing entirely to say, "God is good *because* ...." The key word here is "because," which gives reason to the reality.

---

19 Isa 53:5; paralleled in 1 Pet 2:24.
20 This points us forward to a similar point made in Rev 12:11.

The actions of God stem from His character. He is not inconsistent, like us, who oftentimes act against our very identity. The activity of God affirms what is already true of Him and what has *always* been true of Him. Because of this, we can worship Him with great confidence and delight.

The Multicultural People of God

The language of Rev 5:9–10 demonstrates a twofold strategy of salvation. First, in 5:9 John refers to a deliverance from sin's penalty and power with language of redemption, stating that Jesus "bought *people* for God with [His] blood." And second, by purchasing a people with His blood Jesus "made them a kingdom and priests" who "will reign on the earth" (5:10). I agree with Leon Morris, "[r]edemption is not aimless; [sinners] are bought so that they may belong to God (cf. 1 Cor 6:19–20)."[21] The verb used to translate "bought" in Revelation 5:9 can also mean "purchase" or "redeem." It is language used to describe the ransoming of a slave. John uses the metaphor in 5:9 to highlight that it was by the death of the Lamb—more specifically, *His blood*—that secured the freedom of His people from their former master.

However, by being set free God's people do not become autonomous creature; their allegiance has shifted from that of slavery to sin to slavery to righteousness (cf. Rom 6:16–23). A vivid example of this transfer of allegiance is clearly seen in the Pentateuch and Israel's exodus from Egypt. Although Israel was ransomed from Egypt by the hand of God, their ransom came with the stipulation that they would be obedient to the laws of God outlined not only in the Ten Commandment, but throughout the Torah.

As believers in Christ, we are purchased *by* God, *for* God. It is the salvific work of the triune God for the enjoyment of fellowship with God and with His people. But unlike slavery under a ruthless taskmaster, being God's possession is the source of infinite benefit and blessing. He never exploits His subjects. We are purchased by the blood of Christ, to be members of God's family.

Along with redemption, John refers to a reorienting of a

---

21 Leon Morris, *Revelation*, 100.

believer's social status. The transformation into a kingdom of priests is not a new promise given to believers in Christ, but is instead a fulfillment of the promise Yahweh first made to Israel at Sinai. While on Sinai, God promised that if Israel kept the covenant they would "be a treasured possession ... out of all the peoples ... kingdom of priests and a holy nation" (Exod 19:5–6).

In Exod 19:6, the Septuagint says that God's people will be "kingly priests." Mounce concludes that the promise made at Sinai "is fulfilled in the establishment of the church through the death of Christ. Corporately believers are a kingdom, and individually, they are priests to God."[22] "As a kingdom," Osborne writes, "they form the people of God, the new Israel experiencing a new exodus."[23] This is affirmed in Peter's first letter, where he refers to believers as a "royal priesthood, a holy nation, a people for *God's* possession" (1 Pet 2:9).

The "kingdom and priests" motif encapsulates privilege and responsibility. Our belonging to God compels us to joyful service. Interestingly, God has no need for anything from us. He is unlike the Greek gods who created humanity to serve their needs.

In stark contrast to the Greek Pantheon, Yahweh created humanity to glorify and cherish Him as He takes great delight in us as a people created in His image. We were not made to serve the needs of God but created with an invitation to join the life and love of the Trinity, reigning with God over His good creation. Since the time of the prophet Daniel, God's people have been longing to "take possession of the kingdom forever, forever, and ever" (Dan 7:18, 22).

Although Rev 5:10 refers to the creation of believers into a "kingdom of priests" as already occurring, their reign on earth is something yet still in the future.[24] In light of this, is our duty as "kingly priests" an office we operate in now, or does it remain a role we occupy in the future? The answer to this is the now all too familiar *already/not yet*. And while we currently occupy some aspect

---

22 Robert H. Mounce, *The Book of Revelation*, rev. ed., NICNT (Grand Rapids: Eerdmans, 1977), 136.

23 Osborne, *Revelation*, 115.

24 This is made evident by the use of the future tense βασιλεύσουσιν.

of our priesthood now, there is a far greater fulfillment of this office still in the future. We will revisit the future aspect of our priesthood in when we discuss Rev 22:5 below.

With respect to the present, believers are currently God's royal sons and daughters. God's covenant blessings come with the inheritance of God's mission. The purpose of every believer in Christ is inextricably tied to missiology. Thus, participating in the Great Commission (Matt 28:16–20) is a responsibility tied to our privileged relationship as followers of Christ.

Psalm 82:8 provides a helpful backdrop to the expectation that God's people will be multiethnic. It reads, "Arise, O God, judge the earth, for You shall inherit all the nations." Because Christ has "purchased" believers "from every tribe and tongue and people and nation," we realize that God's intention has always been to create for Himself a multicultural people with which to make a covenant family.

The implications of this challenges the social barriers of any believer. Racism, unquestionably, has no place within Christianity in any form. Such arguments of ethnic superiority were addressed by Paul in his letters to the churches in Galatia and the churches in Rome. The distinction between Jew and Gentile is categorically irrelevant to the dignity and worth of anyone who belongs to the people of God.

Ear-Shattering Worship

> And I heard every creature that is in heaven and on the earth and under the earth and in the sea and everything in them saying, "To the one who is seated on the throne and to the Lamb be praise and honor and glory and power forever and ever." And the four living creatures were saying, "Amen!" and the elders fell down and worshiped. (Rev 5:13–14)

In Rev 5:13–14 we arrive at the pinnacle of worship in the throne room vision of chapters 4 and 5. The innumerable heavenly host shout their accolades of praise to the triune God in what can only be described as truly ear-shattering worship. It is no wonder that we will one day require glorified bodies, because such activities will require abilities we do not possess in our mortal frames. Our lowly ears could not endure such cosmic praise! The outline of praise in Rev 4–5 is as follows. First, God the Father is worshiped in Rev 4:8–11. This is followed by the worship of the Lamb in 5:8–12. Finally, God and Jesus are worshiped together in harmony (5:13–14). The inclusion of heaven, earth, under the earth, the sea, and "all that is in them" illustrates the extent of God's glory and the responsibility of all creation to give Him praise (5:13). Meanwhile, in heaven the four living creatures as well as the elders affirm the praise of all creation, proclaiming "Amen" as they fall down in worship (5:14).

It is hard not to envision all of creation shaking as took place. The adrenaline rush from this experience must be incomparable! Yet, nothing in our history recorded such an experience. Why is that? Was this all hyperbole? Perhaps. But I think something else is going on. The cosmic worship set transpired, and John was a witness, but human history did not take note of it because (although it happened!) most of humanity is used to blocking out the praise of God. After all, the stars preach a sermon every evening (Ps 19:1–4), and how many people actually join in their proclamation? Part of what the mission of God involves is bringing congruence to His worth and the worship He receives. One day everything that is permitted to be in His resurrected cosmos will worship Him. It will not be a reluctant activity, but an enchanted response to the glory of the Triune Creator and Redeemer.

God and the Lamb

Although is it is common for people to accept the existence of a god and even offer it their worship, the great majority of these people fail to acknowledge the sovereignty of Jesus and the obeisance befitting Him as God incarnate. It is this worship of both God and Jesus, or what Larry Hurtado refers to as "binitarian" worship, that is distinctive to Christianity.[25] Köstenberger rightly affirms this

---

25 Larry W. Hurtado, *Lord Jesus Christ: Devotion to Jesus in Earliest Christianity* (Grand Rapids: Eerdmans, 2003), 134–53.

devotion to Jesus, noting that "Jesus was not treated as an alternative object of worship alongside God. He was included in [the] worship of God."[26] God and the Lamb, "are joined in a way which is characteristic of this book (6:16; 7:9, 10, 17; 14:1, 4; 21:22, 23; 22:1, 3). There cannot be the slightest doubt that the Lamb is to be reckoned with God and as God."[27]

Revelation 5 appropriately ends in worship because it is indeed a coronation ceremony. Not only is Jesus worthy to take the scroll, but He also takes His spot in the center of heaven's throne with God the Father, and it is from the throne God and Jesus reign as King over all creation. The preexistent Lord who appeared to Moses in the burning bush (Exod 3), the one worshipped as Yahweh, humbled Himself to become a man. The Gospels record the journey of Jesus revealing Himself, redeeming humanity, and His resurrection and ascension into heaven. The Son of God is now seated on the throne where He, along with the Father, receive the praises of all creation.

The Wrath of the Lamb

The wrath of God and of the Lamb is unavoidable in the book of Revelation.[28] God's wrath is a necessary action, because God is love. It is only because the Lamb of God is loving that He acts in wrath, as the fierce Lion of Judah, against anyone or anything that opposes the object of His love or the holiness of His character. We can observe a similar dynamic in human terms. Because I have a fierce love for my wife, anyone who would attempt her physical harm would experience my wrath in my commitment to protect her.

Old Testament theology refers to a day when God will come and judge the wicked of the world. Such an event is known in the Old Testament as the "Day of the Lord." Isaiah 63 describes

---

26 Andreas J. Köstenberger, "The Deity of Christ in John's Letters and the Book of Revelation," in *The Deity of Christ*, edited by Christopher W. Morgan and Robert A. Peterson, Theology in Community (Wheaton: Crossway, 2011), 167.

27 Leon Morris, *Revelation*, 102.

28 God's judgment is a central theme in Rev chapters 6–20 and is explicitly stated in Rev 6:16–17.

the Lord's coming judgment. In Isa 63:4 we read, "the day of vengeance was in my heart, and my year of redemption had come" (Isa 63:4 ESV).

In both Isaiah 63 the book of Revelation, the Lord is deeply concerned about justice being served. But unlike humanity, God's justice is redemptive in its purpose. Commenting on Isa 63:4 and the day of vengeance, John Oswalt concludes:

> The reader may reply, what about that word vengeance? Does that not convey a mean spirit of revenge and bitterness? It might if it were by itself, but the parallelism here shows that is not the case. What is the vengeance about? God's hurt pride? No, it is about redemption, about breaking the power of sin and evil so that those who are held in its grasp may go free. This is precisely the point that the Servant/Messiah made in 61:2 in similar words (and one more reason to recognize that all of the work of that person, both salvific and judgmental, is included here). God's purpose in destroying evil is never merely an end in itself. It is always in aid of a larger one, the deliverance of the faithful.[29]

The book of Revelation remarks that Jesus's eyes are "like a blazing fire" (Rev 1:14; 2:18; cf. Dan 10:6), a symbol of His fierce opposition to His enemies. The King on the white horse has fire in His eyes because He is zealous to secure safety for His people. The divine warrior has the "day of vengeance" in His "heart" because He has the salvation of His bride in His eyes. All this describes the Lamb of God, who is also a lion-like King coming to establish His kingdom on earth and destroy any who oppose His rule. This is our Lord, before whom we should tremble in awe, yet whom we should worship in adoration.

No one is able to Him, and no one can overthrow Him and His kingdom. He has ascended to the throne and no one will dethrone Him. The humble incarnate Christ has transformed into the glorified kings of kings! His coronation has granted Him the ability

---

29 John N. Oswalt, *The Book of Isaiah, Chapters 40–66*, NICOT (Grand Rapids: Eerdmans, 1998), 598–99.

to show forth His true nobility. His appearance now is what one would expect from the King of the cosmos—radiating light, as the light and beauty of creation only reflects the majesty of its Creator, and powerful in stature, symbolized by His seven horns (Rev 5) and accompanied by a white horse (Rev 19).

With symbol-laden images, Jesus is shown to be the true warrior-king who comes to lay a final blow to anyone and anything that opposes His rule. While the language of conquering utilized by John is vivid, it is important to remember that something definitive has to occur in order for creation to be fully transformed and eradicated of sin and death.

Paving the Way for the Parousia

Imagine reading a book to someone, perhaps your child or a friend. As you read aloud, it is not that the words are being written as you read them; to think so would be absurd. The words were written on the pages prior to the reader experiencing them in their sequential order. And so, it is with human history. As much as humanity likes to think that the ultimate direction of human history is still uncertain, that is simply not the case. The end goal of human history is already written and contained within the scroll—written by God and carried out by God.

Now we await the Parousia (or the return of Christ), which is the final event separating history from the installation of the new creation.[30]

In Revelation, we witness the unfolding of the story written before the foundation of the world. The Lamb of God is the only one worthy to carry forth as a commander the orders contained within the scroll. The scroll of salvation has been written long before we were born, yet its contents are unfolding before our very eyes.

The majesty of the triune God ought to eclipse any worries that plague our days. Revelation 4–5 provide us with a theocentric (vertical) vision that allows us to see the vanity in any anxiety provoked by what is in front of us (horizontally).

---

[30] For my view of the Parousia, looking at 1 Thess 4:13–18, listen to the *Adventures in Theology* podcast episode number 39.

Charles Wesley writes:

> Still the atoning blood is near, that quench'd the wrath of hostile Heaven: I feel the life His wounds impart; I feel my Saviour in my heart.[31]

Do you experience what Charles Wesley wrote about? Do you "feel the life His wounds impart"? The Lion-Lamb was slaughtered so that humanity can be ransomed. His blood has set us free and pays the price so that we can be made new. The full blessing of resurrection is still yet to come, but it is as certain as Jesus's grave is empty.

The Lamb is unfolding the sovereign plan to take back the earth from the depravity of sinful people, to eradicate the evil, and to move the earth beyond its original creation and into its fullest intention. Ultimate victory was secured by the finished work of the Messiah. God's salvation *of* us does not rescue us away *from* the world but rescues us *to* the world and *for* the world, anticipating the glorious renewal of all the cosmos at the end of human history. What we see carried out in the rest of Revelation is simply the administering of the ramifications of Christ's victory—triumphing over His enemies and ushering in the dawn of the new creation.

The eloquent words of Osborne paint this picture: "Christ has become the Lion, the royal Messiah, by becoming the slain Lamb. His death on the cross is the true central event of human history, and through his sacrifice the paschal lamb has become the conquering ram who will end this world of evil and usher in eternity."[32]

While the Prince of heaven has ascended to the throne, has He ascended to the throne of our heart and affections? As the victorious Messianic King stands at the center of the throne and takes the scroll, He displays how worthy He is. He is worshipped in light of

---

31 John Wesley and Charles Wesley, *The Poetical Works of John and Charles Wesley*, edited by G. Osborn, vol. 1 (Wesleyan-Methodist Conference Office, 1868), 106.

32 Osborne, *Revelation*, 119.

His triumph. How could anyone or anything be worthy enough to stand at the center of our focus? As He prepares to finish the task of justice, promising to return to the world and free it from all evil, sin, and the curse, His eyes blaze with fire and He shines with glory. How can anyone eclipse His majesty? Let us worship the King of kings and Lord of lords! Let us join the chorus of heavenly host and saints in celebrating the coronation of heaven's King!

5

The Wedding of Two Worlds

> *There will never again be an earth "down here" and a heaven "up there."*[1]
> —Grant R. Osborne

ONE OF THE PRESSING questions in ancient Judaism centered on the eschatological nature of creation. Much like in today's world, ancient Judaism was concerned with the eschaton and the fate of the world. Today, these questions are answered not on a theological basis, but rather on ecological and economical terms. Humanity is able to slow the decay and destruction of the world but is unable to completely reverse the decay of the world and the outside universe—of course, such a slowing down would take many centuries before humanity sees any actual results. But while contemporary solutions satiate the modern person, those in the ancient world sought after theological answers for the fate of the world.

Revelation answers this question with an uplifting answer: "a new heaven and a new earth!"

> And I saw a new heaven and a new earth, for the first heaven and the first earth had passed away. (Rev 21:1a)

While those who have died in Christ currently experience the bliss of heaven, heaven is only part of the story. The intermediate state is

---

[1] Grant R. Osborne, *Revelation: Verse by Verse*, Osborne New Testament Commentaries (Bellingham: Lexham Press, 2016), 339.

not a *static* mode of existence—that is to say, it is not the fixed and final destination for believers. There is still a sense of waiting and expectancy, a waiting for the new creation.

Jesus's words in John 14:2—"In my Father's house are many dwellings"—typically are quoted as referring to the eternal state, However, this is a misapplication of Jesus's words. What Jesus is referring to here in his usage of housing in heaven is the intermediate state. The word for "dwelling places" (*monai*) is regularly used in ancient Greek, not for a final resting place, but for a temporary halt on a journey.[2] Once again, heaven is like a train in transit to its ultimate destination—that destination being the new heavens and earth.

Those who have gone on to heaven *are* present with the Lord and experiencing genuine bliss. Nonetheless, they anxiously await the final resurrection and the restoration all of creation. Hoekema posits that for the saints in the currently in heaven, "their happiness [is] provisional and incomplete. For the completion of their happiness they await the resurrection of the body and the new earth which God will create as the culmination of his redemptive work. To that new earth we now turn our attention."[3]

A Kainos Creation

Let us now turn our attention to the consummation of the new creation. As we examine what Revelation has to say about the eternal state, it is important not to seek for answers to questions that are not introduced in John's vision. The eschatological questions introduced in Revelation must be answered on their own terms, aided by the context of Revelation and the broader literature Judaism. Reading Revelation with one eye on the Bible and the other on the winds of change will not produce a proper or responsible interpretation of Revelation.

It is important to keep in mind that there is still much mystery surrounding the eternal state. While Revelation does pull back the

---

2 N. T. Wright, *Surprised by Hope* (London: SPCK, 2007), 162.

3 Anthony A. Hoekema, *The Bible and the Future* (Grand Rapids: Eerdmans), 274.

curtain to reveal some details, it does not throw the curtain wide open. There are some parts we catch a glimpse of, and it is important that we cherish every detail of what is revealed. Somethings we are able to make good biblical conjectures about; others will remain a mystery due to the lack of biblical support.

The following outline highlights how Revelation offers encouragement for the future and the new creation:

God's cosmic new creation (Revelation 21:1–8)
God's global temple (Revelation 21:9–27)
God's escalated Eden (Revelation 22:1–5)

The very first words of the Old Testament speak of the first act of creation: "In the beginning God created the heavens and the earth" (Gen 1:1 ESV). Flash forward to the prophet Isaiah and you notice that he speaks of the radically new and redeemed creation, words bearing a remarkable resemblance to Gen 1:1.: "For behold, I create new heavens and a new earth" (Isa 65:17a ESV; 1 Pet 3:13).

Turning to the text of Revelation, we read the following: "Then I saw a new heaven and a new earth. For the first heaven and the first earth passed away and the sea no longer exists" (Rev 21:1). The word "new," (*kainos*), in this passage is the same word found in the Greek translation of Isa 65:17 mentioned above. This is a fascinating choice of word in that it denotes a "qualitative distinction," promoting a superiority of condition, versus merely being new in terms of time.[4]

The new heaven and the new earth are "new" in that they far exceed and eclipse the previous creation. Commenting on *kainos* in *TDNT*, Behm notes that *kainos* illustrates "what is new in nature, different from the usual, impressive, better than the old, superior in value or attraction."[5] The newness by which the new creation will be marked is perhaps best summoned up by the word freshness. It is the superlative, the highest good, exceptional in quality

---

4 "There is a qualitative distinction between the two world orders. καινός ("new") usually indicates newness in terms of quality, not time." G. K. Beale, *The Book of Revelation: A Commentary on the Greek Text*, NIGTC (Grand Rapids; Carlisle, Cumbria: W. B. Eerdmans; Paternoster Press, 1999), 1040.

5 Johannes Behm, *TDNT* (Grand Rapids: Eerdmans, 1964–76) 3:447.

and condition. "Everything the Lord created at the beginning will be made new at the end."[6]

The heaven that will be made "new" is the layers of atmosphere and the starry expanse that encompasses the universe. The phrase, "heaven and earth," is a biblical merism, a designation constituting the entirety of the cosmos.[7]

Thus, the scope of newness is nothing short of all of creation. Just as Gen 1:1 sums up the creation of all things, Isa 65:17 and Rev 21:1 describe the extension of the new creation to expand out to the entire universe. "New creation is the glorious end of the revelation of God's salvation. It is the supreme goal of early Christian hope."[8] The language of the New Testament is clear that God's saving activity is comprehensive and holistic, not just in terms of the spiritual aspects alone.[9]

There will be no differentiation between the heaven of God's realm and the heaven of our realm. Neither is there a differentiation between the earth as we know it now and the renewed earth that awaits its coming. It is our earth that will be made glorified in newness, just as we ourselves will be glorified in newness. Not only will creation be transformed, creation will also forever remain in a transformed state, enduring in an irreversible freshness and vitality.

A Sea-less Existence

> And I saw a new heaven and a new earth, for the first heaven and the first earth had passed away, and the sea did not exist any longer. (Rev 21:1)

When in discussion about Rev 21:1, people often lament at the

---

[6] J. Alec Motyer, *Isaiah: An Introduction and Commentary*, TOTC (InterVarsity Press, 1999), 450.

[7] Cf. Luke 12:56; Acts 2:19; 1 Cor 8:5; Col 1:16, 20; Eph 1:10; 3:15; Heb 12:26.

[8] Behm, *TDNT*, 3:449

[9] E.g., Matt 19:28; Acts 3:17–21; Eph 1:7–10; Col 1:16–20; Rom 8:19–23; 2 Pet 3:10–13—all of which should obviously imply the restorative rescue of both the animate and inanimate; the visible and invisible creation.

absence of any sea in the new heaven and earth. They note the lack of a sea and are saddened by the fact that there will not be beautiful, recreational oceans in the new world. And as one who currently resides by the ocean, I have sympathy for their sadness.

I remember once an occasion where I was teaching a class on biblical interpretation. In one class meeting I was lecturing on the importance of reading the Bible not *literally*, but by its *literary* genre. In order to illustrate my point, I used this very verse from Rev 21 to help my students understand how sometimes we make the mistake of reading a passage far too woodenly, and by doing so we miss the reading intended by the author. A further example of missing the forest for the trees can be seen in how we apply genres to whole books of the Bible. For example, we would not read Proverbs with the same genre expectations as that of the Gospel of Luke. Each author of Scripture used the genre that best fit its *Sitz im Leben* ("setting in life") in order to communicate his message.

Too often, the book of Revelation is not given enough serious attention or consideration. That is to say, some Christians keep any serious study of the book at arm's length, intimated by its otherworldly message and cosmic symbolism. Sadly, by remaining distant observers of Revelation believers rob themselves of its message of hope and restoration. At the same time, those believers who do take the time to read Revelation, but do so without taking seriously the genre, often times find themselves at the wrong end of an erroneous understanding of the book as a whole. Rather than situating Revelation in a thoroughly apocalyptic Jewish background, one that is informed by the Old Testament, these readers tend to situate Revelation more so in the news headlines of the day.

Revelation is an epistle, a book of prophecy, and apocalyptic literature. Contained within it are hundreds of Old Testament allusions and images, and the constant usage of symbols gives shape and color to its message. The absence of the sea as described in this book is a prime example of symbolism at play within the book of Revelation. Why would John speak of the comprehensive scope of new creation but then randomly throw in a geographical detail about the new world as lacking a sea?

It is important to note what John *does not* say. John does not say that there will be an absence of large bodies of water, but what he does say is that there will be no *sea*. Now, Before you are tempted to close this book and move on, please hear me out. Rather than imposing what we think of as a sea today on the meaning of Rev 21:1, instead, we must try to understand what John meant by his use of sea and what this image refers to in Scripture.

If we remember, Genesis describes creation as good, but it was not a consummated creation. The sea is described as chaotic and wild. Furthermore, consider how God pronounced judgment upon the world in Gen 7. At the sight of worldwide evil (cf. Gen 6:5–7), God brought a worldwide flood up His creation. This same pattern is repeated in Exodus, where God once again used the sea as His weapon of judgment.

While the sea was a literal body of water, what did the sea theologically represent in the Exodus narrative? Consider the following:

> **Separation.** Israel was stuck, enslaved in Egypt and unable to leave and cross the chasm of the sea to the land of promise.
> **Danger.** Crossing the sea could be a task that could very well end up being their graveyard if it was not first miraculously dried up.
> **Chaos.** The sea is unpredictable both in the conditions and the creatures in it!

So, Revelation draws the picture of the sea similar to Exodus; it is a place of separation; a place of chaos and unpredictability, a place of danger; it is a graveyard for the dead. Nevertheless, Revelation is unique in that it presents the sea as the place that evil rises from (Rev 13:1). Or is it unique? How intriguing would it be if the Bible drew a connection between the sea and the evil beast that comes from the sea?

There are a few passages I want to draw our attention to:

> **Exodus 14:21**: "Then Moses stretched out his hand over the sea, and the Lord drove the sea back by a strong east wind all night and made the sea dry land, and the waters were divided."
> **Psalm 74:13**: "You divided the sea by your might; you broke the heads of the sea monsters on the waters."

Both reference the dividing of the sea; but the Psalm talks about a monster at the red sea. Who is the monster?

Ezekiel 32:2: "Son of man, lament for Pharaoh king of Egypt and say to him, You compare yourself to a lion of the nations, but you are like a monster in the seas. You thrash about in your rivers, churn up the waters with your feet, and muddy the rivers."

This passage compares Pharoah to a dragon of the sea! The same Hebrew word (*tnyn*) for "sea monster" is used here and in Ps 74:13, proving there is a connection. But there is more to see.

Isaiah 27:1: "In that day the Lord with his hard and great and strong sword will punish Leviathan the fleeing serpent, Leviathan the twisting serpent, and he will slay the dragon that is in the sea."

Within Isaiah's apocalyptic passage (Isa 24–27), he mentions the fate of the beast of the sea. The monster of the sea will be slain and dealt with. The resemblance between Revelation and Isaiah is remarkable already. Spotting this kind of imagery, where the sea monster is defeated in an apocalyptic, eschatological passage, brings clarity as to its possible usage in Revelation. Turning to Rev 13:1, John introduces his readers to "a beast rising from the sea." By doing so, John gives his readers a better idea of what the beast represents in his argument.

In and of itself, the sea is not inherently evil. However, it is metaphorically communicating the presence of evil that originates within it. It is the source of chaos and conflict. The sea has been a source and battle grounds of hostility and divine conflict for God's people for generations. Thus, when we read Rev 21:1 we have a more robust view of what the sea is. It is not an obscure symbol or image. Rather, the absence of the sea in Rev 21:1 is a reference to the abolition of chaos and evil. This brief survey above does not begin to scratch the surface of biblical examples where the sea functions more than just a body of water.

In Revelation, "sea" (*thalassa*) is used twenty-three times. Each of these uses of sea in Revelation refer to the sea as being the place from which the beast arises out of (13:1), into which Babylon the Great will be thrown into as a place of banishment (18:21), and as a graveyard for the dead (20:13).

It is also important to note that John was banished to the island of Patmos and separated from the churches to whom he wrote. John had the vivid experience of walking onto the shore and gazing across the sea, staring at the vast expanse that had separated him from his church family. In summary, we can gather from the biblical data that the sea is a primary symbol of chaos, the origin of cosmic evil, the place of the dead, and a large chasm separating people from one another.

Be that as it may, there is a peculiar appearance of the sea in Rev 4:6. As we have already noted, Rev 4 pulls back the curtain to reveal God's present as He rules from His throne in heaven. While it is clear from the text that we encounter some rather astonishing imagery, we also note a crystal "sea like glass" before the throne of God. Whether God literally has a "sea like glass, like crystal" at His throne or not is unimportant. What matters is the symbolism that John is communicating by his depiction of the sea before the throne of God. Despite the absolute disorder being visited upon the world as a consequence for humanity's rebellion, God's reality in heaven is one of order, which is noted in the still-like nature of the crystal sea.

There is nothing in heaven that is threatening the peace of God's rule or those in His presence. In His incarnate ministry, Jesus proved to be the true embodiment of heaven on earth as He restored dead or decaying things to life (in His healing ministry) and brought peace to the chaotic forces of this world (in calming the sea and even walking on it). He foreshadowed His divine ability to bring harmony back to a chaotic creation.

With respect to Rev 21:1–22:5, these verses are unique in that they present an exclusively future event, the longed-for eschaton. It is at the eschaton that God's reality in heaven invades and pervades all of creation once again. Not a *single square inch* is untouched by His redemptive power that is "making all things new" (Rev 21:5).

The removal of the sea from the new creation points to the

removal of the chaos of the previous world, along with the removal of the grand graveyard that will no longer be necessary—for all who live on the new earth will never go to the grave. Death will become a distant memory and an eradicated reality.

Anthony Hoekema writes agreeably: "Since the sea in the rest of the Bible, particularly in the book of Revelation ... often stands for that which threatens the harmony of the universe, the absence of the sea from the new earth means the absence of whatever would interfere with that harmony."[10] Likewise, Spurgeon opines, "Scarcely could we rejoice at the thought of losing the glorious old ocean: the new heavens and the new earth are none the fairer to our imagination, if, indeed, literally there is to be no great and wide sea, with its gleaming waves and shelly shores."[11]

Recreation in the New Creation?

We have ample reason to believe that the new earth will contain majestic oceans, lakes, and rivers. The absence of the sea in Revelation is the absence of anything that would threaten life and God's rule (cf. the beast in Rev 13:1). Therefore, watery expenses will still prevail, but without the threat of death. While chaos has plagued human history ever since the fall, the new creation will be characterized by harmony.

I am convinced that our oceans and beaches will be a part of God's new creation and will still be a means to glorify God, but they will be unhindered by the marring of sin. And so, they will continue to serve as a place of recreational activity. I can only imagine what the new Hawaii will look like! I can only imagine what beauties and activities will await us as we dive into the delight of the new oceans. Remember, everything will be *kainos*; it will be new and superior to the first creation.

On our honeymoon, my wife and I had the privilege to go to

---

10 Hoekema, *The Bible and the Future*, 284.

11 C. H. Spurgeon, *Morning and Evening: Daily Readings*, December 19th Reading (London: Passmore & Alabaster, 1896), devotional for December 19, PM.

Jamaica. The months of saving up paid great dividends as we enjoyed the warm sun, delicious food, and the starry nights. Undoubtedly, my favorite activity was snorkeling. (You must realize that my biggest fear is being attacked by a shark, so this was kind of a big deal for me.) As we plunged into the water, we swam among fish of various kinds and colors. The reefs had plants that danced and swayed with the rhythm of the ocean. My snorkeling mask was snug to my face, held tight by the unfaltering smile that so naturally came from such an enchanting hour. Each time I surfaced was an opportunity to exulted God in worship!

Every second, in every movement, I experienced God's presence and goodness, and no one can convince me otherwise. I was communing with God, enjoying His company, and celebrating the work of His hands. It was new, fresh, and refreshing. Life was vibrant, and I was basking in the creation of my Creator. That day, more than any others previous, I learned that recreational activity in God's creation can promote the most fervent and heartfelt worship to God.

I have had a few individuals challenge me on this, saying something along the lines of: "We will be worshiping God in the new earth for all eternity! How does your idea of snorkeling fit into all of that?" I would reply something like this: "I do agree that we will be worshiping God in all we do for all eternity in the new earth. And I believe that includes recreational activities. If you have not learned how to do any activity to the glory of God, then perhaps you have much to learn on how to worship God with more than your voice."

The point I want to make is this: Worship is not only a song we sing, but also a life we live. Everything that is not inherently sinful has the potential to be glorifying to God and pleasurable to us (cf. 1 Cor 10:31). It is even possible to make a scriptural case that Yahweh enjoys His creation. For example, in Job 38:16 Yahweh asks the following of Job: "Have you entered into the sea's sources? Or have you walked around in the recesses of the deep?" Of course, the question is rhetorical. Yahweh is making the case in Job 38–41 that Job is not in a position to understand the ins and outs of God's providence.

Heaven on Earth

And I saw a new heaven and a new earth, for the first heaven and the first earth had passed away, and the sea did not exist any longer. And I saw the holy city, new Jerusalem, coming down out of heaven from God, prepared like a bride adorned for her husband. And I heard a loud voice from the throne saying, "Behold, the dwelling of God is with humanity, and he will take up residence with them, and they will be his people and God himself will be with them. (Rev 21:1–3)

If you have ever watched the show Planet Earth, you will quickly discover how the circle of life involves a constant struggle for survival. It is self-evident that life is not the way it should be. Admittedly, my favorite part of the show is the phenomenal scenery. It shows some of the most gorgeous landscapes nature has to offer, along with the creatures that live in the various terrains. However, the show does not shy away from the fact that nature is both hostile and decaying. Even common recreational activities, like camping in the United States, are not devoid of danger. Whether it be the risk from wild animals, poisonous plants, or from other inherent dangers, there are many ways by which nature is capable of causing humanity serious harm.

I recall an instance in which I found myself in dialogue with a person with an atheistic worldview. During our conversation the topic of God's special love for humanity came up. At this point in our conversation, I was asked rather bluntly, "We have discovered millions of planets throughout the universe, what makes you think Planet Earth is so special?" to which I replied, "Because no other planet is meant to become the home of God." This, of course, required much further explanation, in which we began talking about the cosmological (and eschatological) differences between his perspective and my biblical worldview.

I refer to this conversation because some Christians may be tempted to scoff at my answer to his question. They might say something like, "Surely God will not live on earth! He lives in heaven!" But that is precisely my point! Heaven is only heaven because

God is there. But earth will become *heaven*, too, because God will make His dwelling *here*. That is the wonderful truth behind Rev 21:3. The home of God and the home of humanity will be one and the same. Hoekema concurs:

> The "new Jerusalem"...does not remain in a "heaven" far off in space, but it comes down to the renewed earth; there the redeemed will spend eternity in resurrection bodies. So, heaven and earth, now separated, will then be merged: the new earth will also be heaven, since God will dwell there with his people. Glorified believers, in other words, will continue to be in heaven while they are inhabiting the new earth.[12]

According to Scripture, heaven is the abode of God; it is where God dwells. So, when Rev 21:3 says that the "dwelling of God" will be with humanity, it is saying that heaven itself will be with humanity. The life of heaven and the life of God are the same thing. Matthew's Gospel goes as far as using the phrases "Kingdom of God" and "Kingdom of heaven" as synonyms.

When read "happy are the meek for they shall inherit the earth" (Matt 5:5), we have to remember that just two verses earlier, the "poor in spirit" are "happy" because "the kingdom of heaven belongs to them." It is not that the *poor in spirit* and the *meek* inherit different places, for such an interpretation is absurd! The poor in spirit *are* the meek, just described by different verbiage. Thus, all the "rewards," per se, in the Beatitudes are different pieces of the same puzzle. To possess the "kingdom of heaven is the same as inheriting the earth, in the sense that the destiny of the kingdom of heaven is to come down and marry the earth.

For the first time ever, God's permanent residence will be with His people (Rev 21:3). The two worlds, for the first time, will be wed—joined in a holy matrimony—sealed by a new and permanent covenant between God and creation. The realm of God and the realm of humanity will intersect, becoming inseparable and indistinguishable.

---

12 Anthony A. Hoekema, *"Heaven: Not Just an Eternal Day Off,"* Christianity Today (June 6, 2003), http://www.christianitytoday.com/ct/2003/122/54.0.html.

God's love, goodness, power, and beauty will touch every part of His marred creation, making it new. There will be no aspect of the universe that is not heaven, since the entirety of creation will be captivated by the presence of the triune God.

> From verse 3 [Rev 21:3] we learn that the dwelling place of God will no longer be away from the earth but on the earth. Since where God dwells, there heaven is, we conclude that in the life to come, heaven and earth will no longer be separated, as they are now, but will be merged. Believers will therefore continue to be in heaven as they continue to live on the new earth.[13]

Heaven and earth will be indistinguishable and inseparable. Said more provocatively, heaven will be earth, and earth will be heaven. Grant Osborne hits the nail on the head when he concludes: "There will never again be an earth 'down here' and a heaven 'up there.'"[14]

Of course, this does not mean that heaven is literally above us while the earth rests below it. The ancient understanding of heaven residing "above" is metaphorical, describing the higher form of life associated with heaven. It is akin to when someone receives a promotion at work—it does not mean that they necessarily move to an office on the next floor above. Such an understanding of heaven would be missing the point.

Romans 8, which speaks about the Christian's release from condemnation, include verses that speak of creation's eventual release from the curse of sin. Verses 21 and 22 demonstrate that all aspects of creation await the effects of redemption. God's "making all things new" (Rev 21:5) applies not only to people, but also to creation. In Rom 6:18, 22, and 8:2, the verb for "set free" is used, applying to human freedom from sin's penalty and power.

Romans 8:21–22 reminds us that even the physical nature needs more than a makeover; it needs to be made new. The vivid language describes a creation that is frustrated because it cannot

---

13 Hoekema, *The Bible and the Future*, 285.
14 Osborne, *Revelation*, 339.

become what it was destined to be. That is why even the most *beautiful* sunset you see is still a *broken* sunset, marred by sin, still in bondage to the curse upon all creation, awaiting the effects of redemption.

If Rom 8 teaches us anything, it demonstrates that creation and humans share twin destinies. Where humanity fell, so did nature. And When humanity is glorified at the eschaton, so all the cosmos will be, too. In sum, humans and creation were created for an intrinsic, mutually beneficial relationship where the flourishing of one culminates in the flourishing of other. There is no way to imagine the resurrection of believers without the pairing of a resurrected cosmos.

Our current predicament is one of chaos and danger. That is why Rev 21–22 presents such an incredible solution to our current condition, because it is counterintuitive to what we know as the normative for human existence. God is, indeed, going to make His home with us and administer on earth the very life of heaven.

It is not just that God will apply the life of heaven to our world. Much more than that, He will bring heaven down to earth! God the Son has already condescended to humanity in the incarnation to redeem humanity. That was when the purchase was made. Now, at the second coming, the kingdom of heaven will descend and permeate all of creation.

Heaven and earth will be joined as one—a marriage between two realities. There are two eternal marriages that will one day be consummated: one between heaven and the earth—forming a whole new creation; the other between Christ and the Church—forming a whole new relational intimacy.

Likewise, note the covenant language of Revelation 21:3. It is as if vows are being exchanged between God and humanity: "They will be His people, and God Himself will be with them as their God." Christ's first descension from heaven was to save people for God; His second descension from heaven will be to bring the life of heaven down to earth (cf. Heb 9:28). Just as Christ intends to wed His people, He also intends to wed His two worlds. It cannot be said enough: *The eschaton is the wedding of two worlds.*

The Death of Death

> And he will wipe away every tear from their eyes, and death will not exist any longer, and mourning or wailing or pain will not exist any longer. The former things have passed away. (Rev 21:4)

There is nothing in all of human experience that levels the playing field like that of death. Death is the great equalizer of all people—it is the respecter of no one! Death comes for the rich just as surely as it comes for the poor. This is the message of the Psalmist in Ps 49, where the social status of one's life is of no value when death comes knocking. As the Psalmist states, "For when [a rich person] dies he will carry nothing away; his glory will go down after him" (49:17). Death is a no doubt a dreadful thing, and no matter how many times humanity tries to find ways to advert its appearance, we will never be able to conqueror its inevitability.

There is something so mysterious about "what comes next." I once was camping somewhere so dark that without a flashlight you could not see your own hand in front of you. That is how many people feel about death; it is a dark, unknown place in which we cannot see what is ahead of us. Francis Bacon was right: "Men fear death as children fear to go in the dark."

Christians should have a peculiar confidence toward death. Instead of fear, Christians can embrace death with immense joy, knowing that Jesus has promised eternal life to those who trust Him (John 11:25–26). Our resurrected King defeated death when He walked out of the grave—though we await its final eradication at the eschaton (cf. 1 Cor 15:26). Not only is death defeated, but it is also "abolished" (2 Tim 1:10).

While Jesus was certainly raised by God the Father, He also takes the credit for raising Himself from the dead. In John 2:19, Jesus speaks in the active voice in the Greek, meaning that He anticipated performing the action of raising Himself from the dead. Why does this matter? Because if we have a relationship with Jesus, then we do not have to be afraid of dying. We trust a worthy Savior who Himself conquered death on our behalf.

So, when God promises that "death shall be no more," we should have no problem believing this to be so. Jesus's resurrection is the assurance that death has been rendered powerless. And one day, death will also die (Rev 20:14), being laid to rest in an unmarked grave in a vacant cemetery. The sorrow of death will become a distant memory, no more than a half-remembered dream. Death will not merely be imprisoned and detained; it will be annihilated and destroyed. Therefore, as Christians we can embrace death as a valley we walk through, a passageway necessary to traverse in order to arrive at the shores of eternity.

Founders of various religions can make all sorts of audacious claims, but each of their bodies is dead in a grave somewhere. Only Christianity has a Savior who walked out of the grave, as He promised He would. Death could not hold Him; the grave could not contain Him. Acts 2:24 goes so far as to say "it was not possible" for death to keep Him down!

The death of Christ is not a mundane loss of life. He drank the cup of God's wrath on our behalf, and even that could not keep Him in the grave. As Paul says in Acts, "You will not permit your Holy One to experience decay" (13:35; cf. Ps 16:10). Jesus was never meant to die to remain dead. Instead of merely His teachings living on after His death, He Himself lives on to rule and to reign from heaven right now, eventually bringing history to its inevitable end and its new beginning.

In Isa 25:8, the prophet prophesies about the day when God would "swallow up death forever." It is quite ironic that death is swallowed up in this passage. Just two verses earlier (Isa 25:6–7), Isaiah sets the stage—or should I say, set's the table—with a vision of a banquet. The passage prophecies an eschatological banquet where Yahweh feasts with those who have trusted in His salvation. Guess what is on the menu? *Death*.[15] The very entity that was epitomized in the Hebrew mind as swallowing people up is now the

---

15 "Isa 25:8 [shows] Yahweh swallowing up Death and this indicates more clearly a parallel with Canaanite mythology: normally it was Mot who did the swallowing, but in this case Yahweh makes nonsense of the law of Canaanite myth by himself swallowing the swallower." J. F. Healey, "Mot," ed. Karel van der Toorn, Bob Becking, and Pieter W. van der Horst, *Dictionary of Deities and Demons in the Bible* (Brill, 1999), 601.

object of the end times feast. Death is not only destroyed, but also feasted on and swallowed up.

However, Isa 25:8 is also encouraging because of how it refers to God as the one that will "wipe every tear from our eyes." The thought of God personally wiping away the tears of our past pain is something so tremendous. We are not innocent in this matter. We have all, at least to some degree, contributed to the world of sorrows. But a day is coming when sorrow, mourning, pain, and ultimately death will no longer exist.

Sadly, there are people who have become too accustomed to the idea of death. If death feels like something so awful, so tragic, so out of place in this world, then *good*! Humanity was not created to die. Thankfully, the consequence and natural repercussion of all sin will one day cease, along with sin itself, never to repeat itself. Until then we are left with the reality that death is not natural. Death is the consequence and wage of sin. Death is the destiny for those who never experience redemption. That is why the final judgment of the unredeemed is called "the second death" (Rev 20:6, 14; 21:8), because it is a second, and permanent, death of the whole person—a terminal punishment and cessation of life.[16]

The eschatological reality according to Rev 21:4 is this: All will be made right, and death will taste the permanent dose of its own medicine. Death will die without any hope of resurrection. And God Himself will be the One to wipe away our tears, comforting us with the knowledge that even suffering has an end, but joy will have a new life and God's love and jubilee will have no end. This is a cause for elaborate celebration—a celebration that should begin in the present.

The truths presented here should be well rehearsed in our church conversations, sermons, and teachings. Frankly, I have a conviction that our discipleship pathways ought to fortify

---

16 "[The 'second death'] in Jewish and Christian thought, both deaths affect the whole person, since belief in bodily resurrection does not allow for separation of mind or soul from the body. The refusal to accept the offer of life leads to the finality of death, symbolized by the destructive power of fire here just as in the teaching of Jesus (Matt. 13:40, 50; Mark 9:48)." Ian Paul, *Revelation: An Introduction and Commentary*, ed. Eckhard J. Schnabel, vol. 20, TNTC (IVP, 2018), 335.

Christians to be ready to die with poise and confidence. That is why I do not see the topic of eschatology as secondary or subordinate to Christian discipleship and faith—it is an integral and vital part of discipleship! The study of eschatology bolsters the foundation of our faith, thus providing a means to flourish! After all, once you take away the sting of death (1 Cor 15:55) there is no longer any fear of the grave.

God with Man

It is difficult to read the first four verses of Rev 21 and not be amazed at how patient God has been in bringing redemption to His people. Although we have just begun our look at the vision of the eternal state, we can gather so far that God truly desires to dwell with us more intimately than the English language can convey.

At the grand finale of redemptive history, we do not find humanity striving to dwell with God. Instead, we see God making His dwelling with His people. His pursuit of us and toward us has been the story of the Bible since Gen 1. It is His prerogative and His initiative. The language in Revelation arises from the echoes of the Old Testament. The Lord says: "And I will walk about in your midst, and I shall be your God, and you shall be my people" (Lev 26:12; cf. Ezek 37:27). There has never been a time when God stopped pursuing us or when human effort eclipsed the work of God to make a permanent home to live with His people. The triune God will one day delight in our company as we, and all the redeemed universe, will delight in His presence.

Have you ever considered enjoying God as the highest aim of human existence? The Westminster Catechism speaks of the highest aim of humanity when it states: "Man's chief end is to glorify God and enjoy Him forever." This implies a constant communion between the human and the divine presence. God's presence with us will be perfect (unveiled in quality), pervasive (comprehensive in scope), and permanent (eternal in duration). This is worth repeating. I call this the "3 P's."

In the new creation the Triune God's presence will be:

Perfect (unveiled in quality). Something that is perfect is the absolute ideal; flawless; it has no room for improvement.

Pervasive (comprehensive in scope). There will not be a spec of creation that is not flooded with God's life, love, and presence. It will cover every square inch of the resurrected cosmos.

Permanent (everlasting in duration) Something that is permanent has no end; it does not fade; it will endure forever and ever.

Putting it altogether now: The establishment of the new creation will bring *perfection, pervasiveness,* and *permanence* to the presence of God with us and all creation.

Although God is "with us," His unhindered manifest existence is not here in its entirety, *yet*. But it *will* be.

For the first time, God will fully and forever make His home on earth where all of creation will feel His presence like never before. Heaven and earth will be joined together. It will be a wedding between the two worlds, where God's space and our space will be one in the same. All of creation will shout with joy at such a cosmic wedding!

What we believe about the future impacts every aspect of how we live now. And I hope it is also clear that what we believe about the future changes everything! Knowing that death will one day *die* and lie in its own grave; knowing that sorrow will cease; knowing that chaos will be no more; knowing all of this, we begin to have our souls awakened to the truth of the eternal plan far greater than anything our world hopes for.

Biblical hope is not irrational optimism. Our confidence that God will finish accomplishing His promise comes from looking back at the whole of salvation history and seeing all that He has done to fulfill His own word. And when Jesus walked out of the grave, defeating the greatest enemy of humanity—sin and death—we can be confident that not only is new creation possible it is also certain.

6

God's Thesis Statement

> *He is the origin and goal of all history. He has the first word in creation, and the last word, in new creation.*[1]
>
> —Richard Bauckham

Part of effective writing is learning how to compose a clear thesis statement. If done properly, a successful thesis statement will inform the reader of the theme that will encompass the writing. The entirety of the writing will serve to defend, expand upon, and clarify what is presented in the thesis statement.

In the case of the Bible, I would suggest that there is one central theme running through the pages of Scripture: the goal of new creation. Everything in the Bible contributes to the thesis of new creation: demonstrating the need, describing the process of redemption, and promising the finished product of God's future work culminated. And because the Bible is God's story, He has both the first and the last word. He is the "author of life" (Acts 3:15). He is the Composer of the symphony of all of history.

The Thesis of Redemption

> And the one seated on the throne said, "Behold, I am making all things new!" And he said, "Write, because these words are faithful and true." (Rev 21:5)

---

[1] Richard Bauckham, *The Theology of the Book of Revelation* (Cambridge: Cambridge University Press, 1993), 27.

In Rev 21:5, the voice of God—the One who sits on the throne—calls out, "Behold, I am making all things new." This statement encompasses the very heart of the book of Revelation and, I would venture to say, the very heart of the whole Bible. If we were looking for a thesis statement of God's redemptive work, we should perhaps look no further than Rev 21:5.

The message of Scripture can be summed up as an eschatological journey from original creation to new creation. The emphasis I wish to highlight is God relentless pursuit of his creation—at no point does God give up on His creation! Salvation *must* involve saving His creation, not discarding it. Everything from Genesis to Revelation serves to accomplish and apply resurrection to the creation.

When I was in high school, I tore the rotator cuff in my shoulder during a wrestling match. It took time and physical therapy, but eventually my shoulder healed. Now when I say it was "better," I mean it was better than when it was first injured. And while I have surpassed the strength I possessed in high school, I will never have the range of motion I once had in my right shoulder before the injury.

Although my experience with a torn rotator cuff serves as an imperfect analogy, it does illustrate what God does with this horribly injured world we call home. God does not take the bruised creation and put a Band-Aid over its wounds; He does not look upon our chronic illness (sin) and simply prescribe painkillers. On the contrary, God takes His creation and transforms it into something new! Our very bodies and our minds—the totality of our being—will experience God's renewal in such a way that nothing else could even add to it. If God were to set out a "suggestions" box after He is finished with us, it would without a doubt remain empty forever! For there will be no way to ever improve upon His salvific gift.

The other noteworthy quality of God's new creation is that it stays *new* and *fresh*. If the eternal God is dwelling with a creation worthy of His infinite glory, and the "former things," such as death and decay, have passed away, then there is no way that life in the eternal state will ever feel "old" or "rusty."

When we think of something new, our concept of this newness is within the realm of perpetual decay. For example, the moment you drive a new car off the lot it immediately begins to depreciate in value. Or how within hours of seeing the latest and greatest blockbuster movie we already find ourselves looking forward to what we saw in the previews. The point is that we, not God, have the wrong category for what new really is. God will be the source and sustainer of the constant newness of life that will mark life in the consummated creation.

The present tense "I am making" does not refer to the present time of the Church age, but it enforces the certainty that the future new creation will occur. It is a "prophetic present,"[2] or a "futuristic present," in which the effects are inaugurated but the culminated fulfillment remains primarily in the future. Osborne writes, "Today there is an inaugurated aspect to this: Every Christian is now a 'new creation' in preparation for the final 'new creation' in eternity."[3] Because God *is* making all things new, our identity as a new creation is both a present reality and a future hope.

The book of Revelation heavily emphasizes the hope we have in the future. However, it is important to note that many New Testament passages do exhort us to live as new humans even now (cf. 2 Cor 5:17). God *is* making all things new. We will see it come to fruition in a spectacular way in the future, far beyond anything we see now, but that does not mean we should live as if we are stuck in a waiting room, bored and unable to make any sort of real impact for eternity.

In Christ, Christians—indwelled and empowered by the Holy Spirit—can live as God's new creation initiated in the world. The ethical implications are massive and swarming. The way we live now should be so drastically different, so holy, so in awe of God that it is as if the very presence of God is always with us—after all, is that not what we claim when we say that the Holy Spirit lives in us?

---

[2] G. K. Beale, *The Book of Revelation: A Commentary on the Greek Text*, NIGTC (Grand Rapids; Carlisle, Cumbria: W. B. Eerdmans; Paternoster Press, 1999), 1052–53.

[3] Grant R. Osborne, *Revelation: Verse by Verse*, Osborne New Testament Commentaries (Bellingham: Lexham Press, 2016), 342.

By this point it should be clear that God's new creation will be superior in quality to anything we experience now. Moreover, we have noted that there will be continuity and discontinuity to what we currently experience. But how should we make sense of all of this?

In the final book of the *Chronicles of Narnia* series, *The Last Battle*, C. S. Lewis describes a scene in which Lucy, her family, and her friends are entering Aslan's country (representing heaven), and she begins her journey into the country, saddened to leave Narnia behind. What she sees next surprises both Lucy and the reader:

> "Those hills," said Lucy, "the nice woody ones and the blue ones behind—aren't they very like the southern border of Narnia."
>
> "Like!" cried Edmund after a moment's silence. "Why they're exactly like. Look, there's Mount Pire with his forked head, and there's the pass into Archenland and everything!"
>
> "And yet they're not like," said Lucy. "They're different. They have more colours on them and they look further away than I remembered and they're more…more…oh, I don't know…"
>
> "More like the real thing," said the Lord Digory softly…
>
> "Narnia is not dead. This is Narnia."[4]

Lewis brilliantly refers to the present world as "the Shadowlands," as it foreshadows what is to come. I think of Lewis's story as the best explanation of the *continuity* and *discontinuity* between the current world and the new world to come. We will experience a world so perfect; we will no longer have ambitions greater than our reality; thus, we will be able to be perfectly present, never longing for a better life.

My Imagination Ceased

I know not, oh, I know not, what joys are waiting there, what radiancy of glory, what bliss beyond compare![5]

---

4 C. S. Lewis, *The Last Battle* (New York: Collier Books, 1956), 168–71.
5 Bernard of Cluny as quoted in Brooks, *The Lamb Is All the Glory*, 189.

As I write this, I am sitting at the cliffs of the central coast in California. This part of the country is a popular retirement spot due to its mild climate and breathtaking views. Taking it all in there provokes a paradoxical feeling welling up inside me. Simultaneously, I am both content but not complacent, satisfied but wanting much more than any experience on this side of life can offer. As silly as it may sound, I would like to jump from this coastal-cliff edge and soar among the birds, then dive deep into the ocean blue.

Why is it that even in some great moments—even in the best moments of our lives—there is a sense that nothing in this world can ever satisfy the longings of our innermost being? Is this why we are so captivated by movies or television series? For a few short and fleeting hours we can allow our imaginations to run wild as we live vicariously through fictional or nonfictional characters. One day, we will not need epic cinematography to entertain us. We will not need movie theaters to captivate our imaginations.

Throughout this book I have argued that the greatest fantasy will one day become a reality for the believer in Christ. One day, our longings and imaginings for something more will cease. How astounding is that? Right now, we have the capacity to imagine something better, something more— that is how our imagination enhances our lives. But when the consummation of all of God's promises occurs, we will no longer be able to even imagine something better, because we will be living in perfect bliss.

At the eschaton, our imaginations will cease and we will have every inkling of our desires satisfied—and it will never end! I celebrate the words of J. I. Packer when he says, "Hearts on earth say in the course of a joyful experience, 'I do not want this ever to end.' But it invariably does. The hearts of those in heaven say, 'I want this to go on forever.' And it will. There is no better news than this."[6]

While I am thankful for the information we possess on the subject of the coming new world, I am also aware that the Bible does not answer every question we have, just some of the most important ones. We are not given a map or an itinerary of our eternal

---

6 J. I. Packer, quoted in Mark Water, *The New Encyclopedia of Christian Quotations* (Alresford, Hampshire: John Hunt Publishers Ltd, 2000), 470.

home. Yet, Scripture is sufficient. In the meantime, we must patiently wait with exuberant trust, giving our trust over to God, knowing that His idea for heaven is so much better than anything we could ever think of. We can marvel at the mystery, for the time being.

For example, I do not understand what the metaphor of our marriage union with Jesus will look like. I cannot fathom how He will be able to love us all so collectively, yet so individually—so equally, yet so intimately. It is one of those things in which we must have a very rational faith that an infinite God will be able to blow away our finite expectations. Therefore, I echo the prayer of the puritan Samuel Rutherford: "My desire is that my Lord would give me broader and deeper thoughts, to feed myself with wondering at His love."

Wonder is a healthy component of the Christian life that is far too often misplaced or misunderstood. The more we can get lost in the wonder of an infinite God, the more likely we will be effective in beautifying the world around us, specifically through the expansion of the gospel. "For I consider" the apostle Paul wrote, "that the sufferings of the present time are not worthy to be compared with the glory that is about to be revealed to us" (Rom 8:18).

Who Is the Alpha and the Omega?

> And He said to me, "Everything is accomplished! I am the Alpha and the Omega, the beginning and the end." (Rev 21:6a)

The speaker in Rev 21:6 is the one on the throne, God the Father. He declares Himself to be the "Alpha and the Omega," an unarguable title of deity. Alpha is the first letter in the Greek alphabet, while Omega is the last letter. The appellation "Alpha and the Omega" is meant to signify a unity between creation and eschatology. The God who brought the world into existence is the same one who will bring the world to completion. In later rabbinic writings, the first and last letters of the alphabet were used to denote something in its entirety; "to describe God as the Alpha and the Omega is not a restriction of God to only the beginning and the end but is a declaration of the totality of God's power and control."[7]

It would be difficult to imagine a more explicit claim to deity. Jesus claims a triad of titles, all of which are communicating the same thing. Nevertheless, these titles are exclusive to describing the one God of Judeo-Christian faith—Yahweh. So, if Jesus is claiming such titles, He is proclaiming that He Himself participates in the Godhead.

In the Isaiah, the designation "first and last" was used by Yahweh as a title for Himself: "I am the first, and I am the last" (44:6; cf. 41:4; 48:12). By sharing the same appellation with the Father, Jesus unites their ontological identity while remaining distinct in person from the Father. He is not a "second god"; though He is the very same essence as God and shares in the eternal being of God.

In Revelation we see the same proclamation from Jesus, when He likewise refers to Himself as the "first and the last" (1:17; 2:8). As we noted above, this is a description of Yahweh rooted in Isaiah's writings. Regarding the nature of Yahweh in Isa 44:6, Motyer notes that "[a]s first he does not derive his being from any other, but is self-existing; as last he remains supreme at the End."[8] It should be no surprise that Isaiah's attested usage of such titles is usually in the context of Yahweh's boasting about being the Creator and denouncing the idols of the East (cf. Isa 48). Both God and Jesus receive titles indicating they share in the same divine, eternal identity. As Bauckham correctly concludes, the triune God "has the first word, in creation, and the last word, in new creation."[9]

The glory of God filling and satisfying all things in the new creation is the purpose of the first creation. In the eternal state, sin will be forever eradicated. Christ is the means for accomplishing redemption and is the destiny of redemption. He is the creator and the consummator of all things, and to Him will be all the glory!

---

7 Mitchell G. Reddish. "Alpha and Omega," edited by David Noel Freedman, *The Anchor Yale Bible Dictionary* (Doubleday, 1992), 161.

8 J. Alec Motyer, *Isaiah: An Introduction and Commentary*, TOTC (InterVarsity Press, 1999), 312.

9 Bauckham, *The Theology of the Book of Revelation*, 27.

What is Excluded from the New Creation?

Moving ahead to Rev 21:8, we now shift our focus towards the eschatological elephant in the room, the question of hell. By skipping ahead to 21:8, this allows us to end on a rather encouraging note by returning to 21:6–7 after a sobering discussion on the nature of hell.

> But as for the cowards and unbelievers and detestable persons and murderers and sexually immoral people and sorcerers and idolaters and all liars, their share is in the lake that burns with fire and sulphur, which is the second death. (Rev 21:8)

The category of sinners listed in Rev 21:8 can make even the redeemed person squirm. Many Christians easily associate falling short with being guilty of some of the sins listed above. However, the difference between those described in Rev 21:8 and Christians are the patterns that mark their lives—Christians are no longer characterized by the sins that once ensnared them. Rather, they are covered by the blood of the Lamb and filled with the Holy Spirit, both of which ensure a life characterized by sanctification from sin.

Just as the Israelites once painted the blood of a lamb over the doors of their homes, Christians have also placed the Lamb of God's blood over our hearts. The basis of our refuge is the faithful intercession of Jesus, who is both the priest and the sacrifice (cf. Heb 7:23–28). We are saved by our union with Christ, and it is our faith in Christ that joins our person to His.

Furthermore, what makes the eternal state is Edenic is the total absence of sin. If sin were allowed to exist in the new creation, it would result in another fallen world, filled with fallen people. Therefore, God has given us His assurance that this new world will not fall into the state of this present world. The day sin ceases to exist, death will cease to exist also—as they have a tandem relationship and fate. Part of the blessing of the new creation will be the fact that sin will no longer exist.

Not only will sin's presence be banished externally, but it will also be eradicated internally. Everything about us will be ethically purified, with every inhabitant of the new world only contributing goodness to it. There will no scrap of pollution from immorality or evil. There will be no temptation or desire to ever operate in a way that is antagonistic to God's design.

Although judgment and its relationship to the lake of fire is an uncomfortable subject to broach, because of its presence in Rev 21 it is necessary that we engage the topic here. It would be irresponsible to shy away from a topic that is so interwoven throughout the book of Revelation. If we were to consider the portions of Revelation we passed over (i.e., Rev 1-3; 6-20; cf. 21:27; 22:15), it would immediately become evident how ubiquitous judgment is in the book as a whole.

Finally, it is important to keep at the forefront of our discussion of hell and judgment the goodness and fairness of God. We must trust in God's justice, how He administers it, and upon whom He administers it. The nature in God will met out judgment upon all creation will be done in a manner that most glorifies Himself. Be that as it may, before moving on to discuss hell, let us remind ourselves that God does not "delight in the death of the wicked" (Ezek 33:11), but desires that "all to come to repentance" (2 Pet 3:9).

What About Hell?

I know people who claim they want nothing to do with God, but still expect to go to heaven after they die. But why should someone who has no concern for God desire to live eternally basking in His glory of God? Heaven is the abode of God, and where He is, there also will He be eternally worshiped and glorified. Heaven is a dominated by God's prevailing presence. If someone wants nothing to do with God, then that person should want nothing to do with heaven. He is the very center of life in heaven and the recipient of all its worship (cf. Rev 4-5).

If those who oppose God were permitted into heaven, then heaven would no longer be heaven. Instead, it would be plagued by the same issues that our world has been plagued with for millennia. In the end, those who reject God's invitation to live in His kingdom and under His kingship receive their just desserts—autonomy from God. Ironically, that is called "hell." Not only does God reject sin, but sin, by its very nature, rejects God. Thus, like opposing magnets, God and sin repel each other.

As pertains to the duration of hell, there is a lengthy debate that has taken place within orthodox Christianity.[10] The three positions below on the nature and duration of hell each have their nuances. However, it is important to remember that each of these views *can* be held as an orthodox Christian belief. In essence, this topic deserves a much fuller treatment than what is presented. Be that as it may, here is an oversimplification of the three views to be discussed below:

1. *Eternal conscious torment*—where the person will forever be in conscious misery outside of God's presence, with no hope of relief, tormented in a resurrected and immortal body.
2. *Annihilation*—sometimes called "conditional immortality" or "terminal Punishment"—where the person will be destroyed permanently either instantaneously or after suffering for a specified amount of time.[11]
3. *Christian Universalism*—where, in the end, all people will be reconciled to God through Christ, by whatever means necessary and even if not immediately.

For the sake of transparency, I affirm the second perspective, annihilation, (though I like the phrase "conditional immortality" best

---

10 The early church did not seem to have a uniform position or uniform language on this topic. The point is that the various views of hell, including annihilation of the wicked, unending conscious torment of the wicked, and universal salvation all have proponents in the first centuries of the Christian church. For a fuller discussion on the various views see Denny Burk, John G. Stackhouse, et al, *Four Views on Hell: Second Edition* (Zondervan, 2016).

11 I want to note that we must not confuse ourselves thinking that the devil's eternal destiny is the same eternal destiny for the unbeliever. It is possible that Satan could suffer for eternity while unbelievers are to perish. "Whether the second death is complete destruction or everlasting torment is uncertain from Revelation, although for the Devil, beast, and false prophet, it is everlasting (20:10)." Duane F. Watson, "Death, Second," *The Anchor Yale Bible Dictionary*, 111. I, though, do believe the Devil's end is the same of unrepentant sinners—annihilation.

for it). I take this position both for exegetical and philosophical reasons. While I have not always held this position, through the process of trying to formulate ample arguments against it I ended up being more and more persuaded by the view.[12] Wherever you land on this topic, I encourage you to do honest, exegetical research that involves reading proponents on all sides and listening to respectful debates.

I find the plain reading of passages like John 3:16 to juxtapose "eternal life" with "perish[ing]." Likewise, passages in Revelation that refer to the fate of the rebellious seem to be apocalyptic pictures of ultimate destruction, drawing on Old Testament and Second Temple literature. Commenting on Rev 14:11, Ian Paul addresses the most difficult passage in on this topic:

> Though the phrase *smoke of their torment rises for ever and ever* ... has been interpreted as indicating a continual experience of torment (which raises some particular theological problems), this is difficult to sustain in the light of the parallel at 19:3, where in an identical phrase the "smoke from [the city Babylon] rises for ever and ever" (AT). It is impossible to imagine the city being perpetually destroyed; the image must signify the eternal effect of its destruction, rather than an eternal process of destruction (cf. the destruction of Edom in Isa. 34:10). Rest is a frequent description of the quality of life for the saved in the age to come (Heb. 4:1, 11; cf. Matt. 11:28), reflecting the rest of God on the seventh day following six days of work in creation (Gen. 2:2–3). But it constantly eludes those who worship the beast (repeating the link with Re1. $23), despite imperial promises of peace and prosperity.[13]

---

12 I want to thank Chris Date and the *Rethinking Hell* ministry, who have modeled Christian brotherhood across the perspectives, holding to the essentials of the faith, while engaging in thoughtful dialogue on this important topic. Chris Date is a proponent of "conditional immortality," too, but he still gives equal platform for others to voice their perspective.

13 Ian Paul, *Revelation: An Introduction and Commentary*, ed. Eckhard J. Schnabel, TNTC 20 (IVP, 2018), 250–51. He, too, holds to the position of annihilationism.

So, when Rev 14:11 says "there is no rest" for the wicked (no pun intended), it is communicating that they will not receive the ultimate sabbath rest that is promised to believers in Christ. Note that the Greek text has the phrase in the present tense, *ouk echousin anapausin* (i.e., "they have no rest,"), which is best understood as a present tense that extends into the future. They do not have rest, and they will not have rest, since they do not find their rest in Christ. In this context, the Sabbath motif is clear—those who partake and benefit of God's sabbath "rest" are not unconscious. On the contrary, "rest" is about active, conscious, present enjoyment with God, not unconsciousness. So, to not have "rest" would be the opposite. "No rest means no sabbath, no time of renewal, no participation in God's love and life. This is in contrast to the future life of the faithful, shown in the concluding two verses of this section."[14] The key to understanding Rev 14:11 and how it contributes to the discussion of "hell" is understanding the apocalyptic Sabbath motif.

The above was just a single example found within a single passage. Again, this topic deserves a far more detailed treatment than what I can provide here. My hope is that we can agree on this: Rejecting God's invitation of love, as exemplified on the cross of Christ, is the epitome of self-sabotage. By His mercy, God desires to exchange our sin and death for His righteousness and life. The refusal of such has a permanent effect. But God will not override the volition of His creatures—He honors love as a choice and commitment with consequences.

The Father's Love for Us

> To the one who is thirsty I will give water from the spring of the water of life freely. The one who conquers will inherit these things, and I will be his God and he will be my son. (Rev 21:6b–7)

We are all parched beggars before God. Even the wealth of the

---

14 Catherine Gunsalus González and Justo L. González, *Revelation*, ed. Patrick D. Miller and David L. Bartlett, Westminster Bible Companion (Westminster John Knox Press, 1997), 95.

richest or the works of the most virtuous person cannot earn what God offers to us in Christ. It is solely a gift for those who give not their money or deeds, but their trust to God. Our souls are born with a thirst that cannot be quenched by natural means. We are created with a God-sized hole in our hearts that will remain an empty vacuum without Him.

In light of the emptiness our heart experiences, Rev 21:6b is a refreshing reminder that the fountain of life-giving water is accessible to us "without cost." The mistake most people make is assuming that "without cost" means that salvation is cheap. Nothing could be further from the truth. In reality, salvation is costly. Take for example Mark 10:45: "For even the Son of Man did not come to be served, but to serve, and *to give his life as a ransom for many.*" The cost of the believer's salvation was the death of the Son of Man. Therefore, when Jesus says that He gives His life "as ransom for many" (Matt 20:28; cf. Mark 10:45), what he means to say is that *He* is the payment. The sacrifice of Christ is quite literally the price of our release.[15]

The imagery of the "conqueror" in Rev 21:7 is the same found earlier in the letters to the churches (Rev 2–3). Those who conquer are the ones who maintain allegiance to Jesus despite the hostility of a rebellious world. Believers likewise receive the entirety of the eschatological promises of God. This encourages believers that their endurance in faith is not in vain, and that there is a future inheritance coming for those who faithfully endure.

Being united to Christ through faith, we are heirs according to the promise (cf. Gal 3:26–29). These blessings culminate in the realization of the two highest relational roles: receiving Christ as the divine spouse and receiving God as Father. In view here is the blessed relationship we receive in relation to the Father. We become sons and daughters of God. The inheritance we receive is nothing less than the privileged inheritance of the eternal Son of God.

Furthermore, to be "in Christ"[16] marks a spatial union in which

---

15 For a full treatment on this concept, see the classic work by Leon Morris, *The Apostolic Preaching of the Cross*, 3rd ed. (Eerdmans, 1965), 29–38.

16 Cf. John 15:4; Eph 2:6, 7, 10, 13; Phil 1:1; 1 Tim 1:14. The phrase "in Christ" appears ninety-one times in the ESV, not including other phrases that speak of our union with God through the persons of the Trinity.

our person is encapsulated by Christ's person. I like to illustrate what it means to be in Christ the following. When a person is in the ocean, submerged and basking in the water, they partake of the benefits of being in the ocean, like the health benefits of the salt water on your skin. But they can *only* have these benefits if they are immersed in the ocean. In a similar sense, believers can only partake of the benefits and blessings of God if they are in Jesus—immersed and engulfed in Him. What is true of Jesus is likewise true of His followers, because we are "in" Him. "Christ is still God's unique, divine son," as Beale notes, "but those whom he represents receive the privileges of his sonship."[17]

Perhaps the most difficult truth to grasp about our union with Christ and the sonship we receive is the boundless love that is given to us. In Christ, we become the very object of God's divine love. It is not a comparison of whom God the Father loves more Jesus or us; His affection for us is *equal*.

The life we have in the Son of God is the life that He shares with the Father in the unity of the Spirit. We are welcomed into the life and love of the Trinity by God's abundant grace. God's love for believers comes from a love that is rooted and reciprocated in His very ontology. Or, to put it more simply, God loves you with the very same love with which He loves Himself. The love shared between the Father, Son, and Spirit is shared with all who are in Jesus. D. A. Carson explains this love in the following manner:

> "Christians themselves have been caught up into the love of the Father for the Son, secure and content and fulfilled because [believers are] loved by the Almighty himself (cf. Ephesians 3:17b–19), with the very same love he reserves for his Son. It is hard to imagine a more compelling evangelistic appeal."[18]

The reality is that one cannot speak too highly of love that comes from an infinite God. There is no vocabulary that can express or put a cap on the love the Father has for His Son and for those who are in His Son. Words simply fail to do justice to such a thing. In

---

17 Beale, *The Book of Revelation*, 1058.
18 D. A. Carson, *The Gospel According to John*, PNTC (Eerdmans, 1991), 569.

the present age, our feelings are still marred by sin, and the "feeling" comes and goes. But God's love does not shift or change; it is constant even when our feelings are not.

We currently have an imperfect experience of a perfect reality that we are indeed children of God in Christ. However, one day our experience will perfectly correlate with that familial reality. We will finally, fully, and forever experience the love of the Father.

The Eschatological Nature of Resurrection Bodies

Before concluding this chapter, it would be helpful to discuss the nature of our bodies at the resurrection. Within the continuity of things being made new is the biblical promise of resurrected bodies to accompany the new creation. God's redemption is holistic, making every fiber of our being new, both internally and externally.

As amazing as the human body is, we all live keenly aware of its deficiencies. We can be encouraged by what Scripture has to say about receiving a glorified body. In light of this, there are three passages for us to consider as we ponder the nature of our eschatological bodies—Rom 8:23; Phil 3:20–21; and 1 Cor 15.

Beginning with Romans, Rom 8:23 reads, "And not only creation, but we ourselves having the first fruits of the Spirit we even groan inwardly as we eagerly await for adoption as sons, the redemption of our bodies." This verse in Rom 8 is found in the midst of Paul's argument regarding the present suffering of believers and its inability to be compared to the glorious future awaiting them (cf. Rom 8:18). In this verse, believers are reminded that even the goodness of God that is but a foretaste of what is to come—part of which includes the redemption of our physical bodies.

In our physicality, we can worship and enjoy God. In fact, we cannot worship God to the utmost of our ability until we have bodies that will be capable of doing so. In Phil 3:20–21, Paul builds on this idea:

> But our citizenship is in heaven, and from it we await a Savior, the Lord Jesus Christ, who will transform our lowly body to be

like his glorious body, by the power that enables him even to subject all things to himself. (Phil 3:20–21 ESV)

Notice how Paul infers believers are waiting for Jesus to return *here*, to our cosmos, rather than waiting to flee away from God's created universe. Christ our Savior will return to redeem the creation. Paul's theology of "glorified bodies" tells us that our ultimate eschatological future will not be a disembodied existence.

The Greek word behind "transformed" or "changed" (*metaschēmatizō*) is where we get the English concept of metamorphosis. In this transformation (literally: trans = to change; form = form/shape),[19] the bodies redeemed believers are changed into the highest form and intention of human physical potential, as opposed to their current, flawed state. The key here is that they are *changed*, not *discarded*.

Our bodies will be "transformed" to the quality and likeness of Christ's "glorious body." The splendor and radiance of Jesus's body will be ours, too, However, ours will only illuminate glory right back to the one who gave it to us. Jesus's glorified body is said to be "brighter than the sun" (Acts 26:13), and the saints' future bodies are said to be luminaries "like the stars" (Dan 12:3).

Regarding these glorified bodies, Keown concludes: "Believers will have the same type of body as Christ, a spiritual body, 'a physical body renovated by the Spirit of Christ and therefore suited to heavenly immortality.' "[20] This is a fundamental motivator when we talk about enduring until the end. We get to obtain a condition that allows us to enjoy a state of existence that we were destined for but never able to achieve.

The last passage for us to consider is 1 Cor 15. The fifteenth chapter of Paul's first letter to Corinth represents some of the most comprehensive treatment with respect to the resurrection in the New Testament. Verses 12 through 34 speak as an apologetic to the veracity of Christ's resurrection and its implications for everything

---

19 In Greek, *metaschēmatizō* is a compound word means to change shape. Cf. Silva, *NIDNTTE*, 4:116.

20 Mark J. Keown, *Philippians*, edited by H. Wayne House, W. Hall Harris III, and Andrew W. Pitts, vol. 2, *Evangelical Exegetical Commentary* (Bellingham, WA: Lexham Press, 2017), 2:280.

we believe, including our own future bodily resurrection. Paul refers to these resurrected bodies as "heavenly bodies" (1 Cor 15:40). Verses 40–49 continue the contrast between the earthly and heavenly body juxtaposing dishonor and glory; weakness and power; natural and spiritual. The glorified body is sown in "power," in that it is physically superior.

Furthermore, these bodies are "spiritual" in the sense of being Spirit-dominated. They are bodies controlled by the Spirit of God; completely filled by the Spirit of God; created new by the Spirit of God; given life by the Spirit of God; adapted to heavenly existence; controlled by the spirit; and in harmony with God's Spirit. These characteristics do not indicate immaterial bodies, but supernatural ones belonging to the Spirit and to the coming age.

It is important not to fall into the trap of equating "spiritual" to "immaterial"—this would negate one of Paul's primary arguments in 1 Corinthians, especially in chapter 15. The Greek behind the English word "spiritual" is *pneumatikos*. The root of *pneumatikos* is *pneuma*, which is the word for "Spirit" and the name of the third person of the Trinity. Wright's offers a helpful explanation on this point:

> Greek adjectives ending in *-ikos*, do not describe the material out of which things are made, but the power or energy which animates them. It is the difference between asking on the one hand "is this a wooden ship or an iron ship?" (the material from which it is made) and asking on the other "is this a steam ship or a sailing ship?" (the energy which empowers it). Paul is talking about the present body, which is animated by the normal human *psychē* (the life-force we all possess here and now, which gets us through the present life but is ultimately powerless against illness, injury, decay and death), and the future body which is animated by God's pneuma, God's breath of new life, the energizing power of God's new creation.[21]

This has everything to do with the theme of new creation. Our current body is part of the *first* things, while the resurrected body

---

21 N. T. Wright, *Surprised by Hope* (London: SPCK, 2007), 168.

is of the *last* things. Paul is showing us the distinction between *protology* (the first Adam) and *eschatology* (Jesus, the last Adam).

Those who are in Christ reap the benefits exclusive to the Messianic King. Receiving the eschatological blessing is contingent upon the recipient being united to the giver of the blessing; thus, Jesus is the "life-giving Spirit" (1 Cor 15:45).

The section ends with Paul saying with certainty that the believer will bear "the image of the heavenly man" (1 Cor 15:49). This juxtaposition affirms that even Adam's condition was incomplete in that it lacked eschatological finality. Because the image of Adam is inferior to Christ, we can infer that the glorified bodies of those who are in Christ at the resurrection will be superior to Adam.

It is difficult to know for certain how we will use our resurrection bodies. What are the activities of the new world? We are not given a brochure. We can make educated inferences, but ultimately, we have to trust that God has for us a physical existence of purpose and delight far beyond what we could comprehend. Hoekema describes the activities of the glorified believer as such: "We shall live to God's praise in glorified, resurrected bodies. On that new earth, therefore, we hope to spend eternity, enjoying its beauties, exploring its resources, and using its treasures to the glory of God."[22] We will need *resurrected* bodies to engage in the activities of the *resurrected* universe.

I also concur with Spurgeon's memorable words on the topic:

> Whatever are the characteristics of the Saviour's glorified body, they are to be the characteristics of your body also. You are to have an immortal body, a spiritual body, a body incapable of pain, and suffering, and decay, a body which shall be suited to your emancipated spirit, a body having a wider range than this limited earthly sphere, having greater powers of locomotion, perhaps flying, swiftly as light, from world to world, or possibly having the power even to outrun the lightning's flash. I do not know how wondrous Christ's glorified body is; but I do "know

---

22 Anthony A. Hoekema, *The Bible and the Future* (Grand Rapids: Eerdmans), 274.

that, when he shall appear, we shall be like him (even in body); for we shall see him as he is. (1 John 3:2)[23]

If I were allowed to speculate beyond what is scripturally explicit, I would predict that our bodies will not be marked by physical limitations. Beyond lacking physical decay and frailty, I believe our glorified bodies will have a radiant beauty and physical abilities far beyond what they do now. Like Spurgeon, I do not think flying is out of question. I do not think hours and hours spent below water will be impossible (not that we will even measure time like we do now).

The key to understanding our future resurrection bodies is to look at Christ's resurrection. Something that was literally impossible has become *possible*, and even *promised* to believers, through the resurrection of the Lord Jesus. Through Christ's resurrection, the triune God is going to flood the entire creation—believers, planets, mountains, plants, etc.—with resurrection power, thus bringing glorious newness to everything.

Resurrection in the Jewish-Christian background always involved new, glorified, immortal bodies that would inhabit and rule a new, glorified, resurrected world. *In the new creation we become, by God's power, more than Adam ever was, and this world will become more than Eden ever was.*

---

23 C. H. Spurgeon, "The Christian's Manifestation," in *The Metropolitan Tabernacle Pulpit Sermons*, vol. 52 (Passmore & Alabaster, 1906), 439–40.

7

The Most Holy Place

> *The enjoyment of God is the only happiness with which our souls can be satisfied...Fathers and mothers, husbands, wives, or children, or the company of earthly friends, are but shadows; but God is the substance. These are but scattered beams, but God is the sun. These are but streams. But God is the ocean.*
>
> —Jonathan Edwards[1]

THE SUN'S RAYS ARE GOOD for us, in moderation of course. Healthy amounts of exposure to the sun allow one to receive vitamin D, which helps to absorb the calcium that is essential for healthy bones. Not only that, but the sun's rays can enhance people's moods, thus decreasing symptoms of depression. The chemical that is produced from sun exposure can even help prevent various sorts of cancer! I am lucky to live in Sun-Diego (that is, San Diego, California), where we get plenty of sunshine.

However, we must also be cautious not to overstay our welcomed exposure to the sun. It is recommended that if one plans on being exposed to sunlight beyond fifteen minutes that they wear some type of sunscreen. Too much sun can greatly increase the chances of skin cancer. Too much sun can also harm the immune system. To summarize, the sun is both necessary and dangerous. I

---

1 Jonathan Edwards, "The Christian Pilgrim," in *Sermons and Discourses, 1730–33*, The Works of Jonathan Edwards Series, vol. 17, edited by Mark Valeri. (Yale, 1999), 437–38.

mention all of this because it provides a helpful illustration for us for what follows.

To be in God's presence is the very essence of life itself. Created in the image of God, we are completely dependent upon Him for our very sustenance. Not only are we satisfied physically in the presence of God, but we also find our emotional satisfaction there as well. This is noted in Ps 16:11, where the psalmist declares that "In [God's] presence is the *fullness of joy*." The word used for fullness (Hebrew, śbaʿ) here denotes total satisfaction or abundance. In the presence of God, one's joy is filled up to the extent that it can be filled.

Like our experience with the sun's rays, we absolutely need exposure to God's presence, but unfortunately, with the reality of sin in our lives, we cannot be in God's full presence. A sinful person cannot stand in the full glory of God's presence; that person would be obliterated by God's powerful, dangerous, and fatal presence.

With all of this in mind, the goal of this chapter is to better grasp the sacredness of the new Jerusalem, where God's presence will be unveiled as a place of blessing and everlasting joy.

The New Jerusalem: A People and a Place

> And one of the seven angels who had the seven bowls full of the seven last plagues came and spoke with me, saying, "Come, I will show you the bride, the wife of the Lamb." And he carried me away in the Spirit to a great and lofty mountain, and showed me the holy city, Jerusalem, coming down out of heaven from God, that has the glory of God. Its radiance is like a precious stone, something like a jasper stone, shining like crystal. It has a great and high wall that has twelve gates, and at the gates twelve angels, and names written on the gates which are of the twelve tribes of the sons of Israel—on the east, three gates, and on the north, three gates, and on the south, three gates, and on the west, three gates. And the wall of the city has twelve foundations, and on them are twelve names of the twelve apostles of the Lamb. (Rev 21:9–14)

The Most Holy Place

It is easy to get confused when reading this passage. Once again John employs the use of metaphor to illustrate his point. Case in point, how is the bride of the Lamb now a city that is descending out of heaven? It appears that the heavenly city is both a people (the bride of Christ) and a place (the new Jerusalem).

The "new Jerusalem" is first referenced in Rev 3:12, where all believers obtain the inheritance within the "new Jerusalem." Jesus states in that same verse that this city will come down *from* heaven, matching the description of what will take place in Rev 21:2.

The idea of a new Jerusalem is not foreign to the rest of the Bible, since most of the imagery in Revelation is rooted in something promised in the Old Testament. Note in Isa 65:17 one of first announcements of the future promised new heavens and new earth. Further, 65:18 declares: "I am about to create Jerusalem as a source of *rejoicing*, and her people as a source of *joy*" (emphasis mine). Dwell on that for a moment: God is making a place and a people to be marked by happiness! I find Ortlund's comments on Isa 65:18 to be most helpful: "In the end, there will be only one commandment for God's servants to obey forever and ever: 'Be glad and rejoice forever in that which I create.'"[2]

Moving on, in Isa 65:19 God declares: "I will shout in exultation over Jerusalem, and I will rejoice over my people." It is easy to imagine that we could celebrate with sheer delight what God has done and will do. However, to think that *God* will rejoice in *us* borders on the absurd! How can we bring any pleasure to the Lord? Such knowledge should not cause us think highly of ourselves. Instead, it should show us how great God is, that He would take delight in us.

The relationship between God and His people is mutual in the common joy shared However, this is exclusively due to the redemptive work of God. The entirety the believer's blessing comes from God as the divine-blesser. He receives all the credit and glory for the good that believers receive as the people of God.

What we are attempting to do here is establish that the new Jerusalem is indeed a city, but a city that is both a people and a

---

2 Raymond C. Ortlund Jr. and R. Kent Hughes, *Isaiah: God Saves Sinners*, Preaching the Word (Crossway, 2005), 445.

place. Regarding this bifurcation, Osborne helpfully clarifies, noting that "the new Jerusalem is not only a place but also a people. The city of God is the place where the saints will live for eternity, yet it is wholly composed of the people themselves."[3] As a people, the new Jerusalem is God's collective community of the redeemed brought forth from every tribe, nation, and tongue (Rev 7:1-9). Included in this collection of people are the very ones who were thought to be excluded from God's family, the Gentiles. However, even those who were at one point not God's people are now called "sons of the living God" (Rom 9:24-26). The Gentiles are now welcomed into God's covenant family through faith. Paul goes so far to label all who are in Christ as "Israel of God" (Gal 6:16), authenticating that salvation is not based on ethnic origin (race), but on faith in Jesus (grace). Thus, the new Jerusalem has no basis in the ethnicity humanity—all who believe in Christ through faith "are sons of Abraham" (Gal 3:7).

Even further, "the New Jerusalem is at once paradise, holy city, and temple. As paradise it is the natural world in its ideal state ... as holy city, it fulfills the ideals of the ancient city, as the place where heaven and earth meet at the center of the earth ... in which people live in ideal theocentric community ... as temple, it is the place of God's immediate presence."[4]

All throughout Revelation, Jewish terminology is used to speak both of God's redeemed people from all over the globe, and of God's eschatological promises, maintaining a sort of continuity between the old and new covenants. We must remember that the first Christians (accurately) saw themselves as the *fulfillment* of Judaism in Christ. This should make us comfortable in embracing the Jewish language in Revelation, and elsewhere in the Bible, because as Christians we are the true recipients of the promises of God, since Jesus is the single beneficiary of all the covenant promises and blessings.

The vision includes a brief but important allusion to God's "mountain" (Rev 21:10). Humanity has always viewed

---

3 Grant R. Osborne, *Revelation: Verse by Verse*, Osborne New Testament Commentaries (Bellingham: Lexham Press, 2016), 345.

4 Richard Bauckham, *The Theology of the Book of Revelation* (Cambridge: Cambridge University Press, 1993), 132.

mountaintops as places to aspire to reach. Both innate in humans and in biblical language, mountains play a significant role in eschatology. Ever since Moses first ventured up Mount Sinai, mountains have been associated with the presence of God—this is also true across the religious landscape of all the ancient Near East as well.

In the ancient Near East, temples were almost exclusively constructed on top of the highest place topographically available, so they would be closer to heaven.[5] This indicated the symbolism of ascension, or heights, pertaining to the nearness to God (or the "gods," in pagan views) and His heavenly abode. Jewish literature anticipated that God's eventual mountain dwelling place would be on "the highest of the mountains" (Isa 2:2). This corresponds with Ezekiel's vision of the new temple (Ezek 40:2) and transportation to a "very high mountain." In summary, a mountain is "where heaven and earth meet."[6] Where the tops of mountains literally begin to penetrate the atmosphere (or heaven by one of its meanings), the new Jerusalem descends upon the heights of mountains (showing that the city comes to us), and suddenly the "place where heaven and earth meet" becomes the vantage point to watch in awe as cosmic renewal happens before John's very eyes. These observations harmonize with the conclusion of our previous chapters, in which heaven, as God's reality, permeates our reality and provides eschatological, fresh life to the cosmos.

In Rev 21:11, John draws special attention to jasper, which is emblematic of the glory of God. As noted in Rev 4:3, jasper describes the appearance of the one sitting on the throne of heaven. Jasper, like diamond, is clear and transparent, with a glistening appearance. The symbolism, represented by jasper, communicates much about the future glory of the church. Richard Brooks writes, "The glory of God is at last imparted to the glorified church and thoroughly reflected in her.... The church is adorned with the glory of God, radiated with it, filled with it—aglow with it!"[7]

---

5 Gary V. Smith, *Isaiah 1–39*, edited by E. Ray Clendenen, NAC (Broadman & Holman, 2007), 129.

6 James L. Resseguie, *The Revelation of John: A Narrative Commentary* (Baker Academic, 2009), 34.

7 Richard Brooks, *The Lamb Is All the Glory*, Welwyn Commentary Series (Evangelical Press, 1986), 185.

The new Jerusalem shines with the radiance of the glory of God's presence. And all the inhabitants of the city shine because they are captivated by the light of the Lord of glory. "The Lord of glory," Dennis Johnson exults, "indwells his people and floods his new community with the beauty of his holiness."[8] The radiance of the city is nothing less than the outward beauty of infinite joy secured forevermore.

The foundation of the city, with the names of the "twelve apostles of the Lamb," alludes to the temple vision in Ezek 48:30–35, where the twelve tribes are mentioned. By alluding to Ezekiel's temple vision, John is emphasizing that the grand vision from Ezekiel includes the old and new covenant believers. John's vision is in no way a rejection of ancient Israel. Rather, it is the fulfillment of God's original intention to form a conglomerate of people from all backgrounds united under a single covenant.

God's Global Temple

And the one who spoke with me was holding a golden measuring rod in order that he could measure the city and its gates and its wall. And the city is laid out as a square, and its length is the same as its width. And he measured the city with the measuring rod at twelve thousand stadia; the length and the width and the height of it are equal. And he measured its wall, one hundred forty-four cubits according to human measure, which is the angel's. And the material of its wall is jasper, and the city is pure gold, similar in appearance to pure glass. The foundations of the wall of the city are adorned with every kind of precious stone: the first foundation jasper, the second sapphire, the third chalcedony, the fourth emerald, the fifth sardonyx, the sixth carnelian, the seventh chrysolite, the eighth beryl, the ninth topaz, the tenth chrysoprase, the eleventh jacinth, the twelfth amethyst. And the twelve gates are twelve pearls, each one of the gates was from a single pearl. And the street of the city is pure gold, like transparent glass. And I did not see a

---

8 Dennis E. Johnson, *Triumph of the Lamb: A Commentary on Revelation* (Philippsburg; NJ: P&R Publishing, 2001), 309.

temple in it, for the Lord God All-Powerful is its temple, and the Lamb. (Rev 21:15-22)

The stones mentioned in Rev 21 are not arbitrary; John was not only seeing something, but he was communicating something to his audience. The objects seen have a history of meaning to the ancient audience. As part of their priestly vestments, Jewish high priests wore two onyx stones on their shoulders. Engraved on these stones were the names of the twelve tribes of Israel (Exod 28:9-12). Also included in the priestly wardrobe was the breast piece of judgment. Just as with the onyx stones, each of the twelve stones included in the breast piece were meant to represent the tribes of Israel (Exod 28:15-30).

Not only were the stones meant to represent the twelve tribes, they also were an allusion to Eden. According to Ezek 28:13, onyx was a stone that was found in the garden of God. It was last seen in Eden, but where else do we find? On the foundations of the walls of the new Jerusalem, in the new Eden (Rev 21:20). God intentionally clothed the high priest, His representative for His people, with symbols of the very land they had lost but looked to regain. The Lord encouraged His people with a memorial stone of the past, pointing them toward their promised future.

In Exodus, we learn that God allowed Moses to dwell in His presence in a unique way, unlike the rest of Israel. In one instance, Moses's face radiated as he left Mount Sinai and went back to the Israelites. Moses learned that God planned to have His presence with His people dwell in a mysterious tabernacle. Moses received the pattern, and Aaron became the first official high priest over Israel. Hundreds of years later, the prophet Ezekiel was taken up to the high mountain of the Lord, and an angel with a measuring rod showed him the dimensions for God's new temple (Ezek 40:1-4).

In John's vision in Rev 21, the measurements of the holy city formed a perfect cube. This is not to say that the city is a literal cube, for John's audience would have recognized that this cubed pattern follows the layout of the holy of holies, the most sacred spot in Israel's temple. Like the description given in the book of Revelation, the physical dimensions that were shown had symbolic meaning behind them. Both in the Moses's tabernacle and in the temple that followed, only the holy of holies had dimensions that formed the shape of a cube.

Revelation mentions a measuring rod of "twelve thousand stadia" (Rev 21:16). Like many parts of this apocalypse, this measurement is not to be taken literally, but it shows that the city is massive.[9] The city itself would be an astounding 1,500 miles, covering the entire ancient Mediterranean world. What this staggering sweep of land highlights is a global temple, one that is large enough to host the redeemed from every generation and every nation.

Both the tabernacle and the temple in the Old Testament were faint previews of the eventual, eternal dwelling place of the Lord with His people.[10] The temple represented God's presence with His people, but in the eternal state the entirety of the new creation will be a temple. Further, God and the Lamb will be the temple (Rev 21:22). Intriguingly, in other passages, Christians, themselves, are called God's temple (1 Cor 3:16–17).

If one reads 1 Kgs 6–8 (which contains the building of the temple by King Solomon) in its entirety, you will notice a few things; chief among these would be Solomon's hope to have the temple be a place of prayer. Prayer is the communication between the God and man. Prayer recognizes God's immanence among us (He hears us, and thus He is in a sense present among us), while acknowledging His transcendence far beyond us (He is in heaven, but we are on the earth).

The tabernacle, and then the temple, were viewed as a model, or a microcosm, of the cosmos. To summarize one of the chief purposes of the temple from an Old Testament perspective, I would say this: *The purpose of the temple was to be a place of intersection between God and man; heaven and earth; life above and life below.*

---

[9] Beale says, "The figurative nature of the number is indicated by the fact that the height of the wall, 144 cubits (= about 216 feet), would be 'hopelessly out of proportion for a city some 1,500 miles high' (= 7,000,000 feet in height, if the 12,000 stadia of v 16 were taken literally)." G. K. Beale, *The Book of Revelation: A Commentary on the Greek Text,* NIGTC (Grand Rapids; Carlisle, Cumbria: W. B. Eerdmans; Paternoster Press, 1999), 1074.

[10] Cf. Ezek 48:35, in which Ezekiel calls the new Jerusalem "The Lord is there."

In other words, the temple acted as a place of mediation between God and His people. N. T. Wright comments:

> We must remind ourselves that, for the Jews, the Temple was where the one true God had promised to make his home. The Temple was the place where heaven and earth were joined together. It was the place you went to meet with God. It was the place of sacrifice, of atonement, the place where you went for festivals because you went to celebrate the presence and love of God.[11]

No Need for a Temple

The means of mediation has been replaced, as the Lamb has taken the Church as His bride, whom He sacrificed Himself to redeem. Thus, no more priestly mediation is needed, because the sacrificial ceremony has been eclipsed by the greatest wedding ceremony of all time.

In the new Jerusalem temples will no longer be necessary, for the eschatological reality of the temple's true meaning has arrived. Wright is correct in his conclusion regarding temple, noting that "[t]he Temple in Jerusalem was always designed, it seems, as a pointer to, and an advance symbol for, the presence of God himself. When the reality is there, the signpost is no longer necessary."[12] God and the Lamb become the realization of all that was symbolized by the Old Testament temple.

Furthermore, one can make the argument that temples have already faded into the background, as is the case with the author of Hebrews. The purpose of the Old Testament temple was to provide a place of propitiation for the sin of God's people (Heb 9:6–7). However, the temple, and more specifically, the holy of holies, was but a symbol of the present time, where gifts and sacrifices were continually offered, but never able to provide the inner cleansing necessary for the complete purgation of sin. The outward

---

11 N. T. Wright, *Following Jesus: Biblical Reflections on Discipleship* (SPCK, 1994), 31.
12 N. T. Wright, *Surprised by Hope* (London: SPCK, 2007), 117.

regulations and washings called for under the old covenant were a stop gap imposed upon the people of God until the time of reformation, a reformation of the inner man through the once for all sacrifice of Christ (Heb 9:8–10).

In a similar vein, the people of God, the Church, are ambassadors of God as His temple presence in the world. Paul makes this point in his second letter to the church in Corinth, stating that "we [believers] are the temple of God" (6:16a). To support this claim, Paul quotes from a number of Old Testament passages that have affinities with the temple and its function as sacred space. Quoting from Lev 26:12 (cf. Ezek 37:26–27), Paul notes that God's presence will be in and with His people: "I will live in them and will walk about among them, and I will be their God and they will be my people" (2 Cor 6:16b).[13] The function of church as an end time temple is one of holiness. As is the case with the temple in Jerusalem, this end time temple of believers is also a sacred space, and as such, it is to be separate from all things unclean (2 Cor 6:17). However, be that as it may, the inaugurated temple presence through the Church still awaits the consummated presence of the triune God Himself.

God's presence will be pervasive in scope, permanent in duration, and perfect in quality—blessing all of creation in an uncanny way unlike any other time in all of history. The glorious presence of the triune God will be, simultaneously, with us, indwelling us, and all around us. Meredith Kline summarizes this, saying: "By virtue of this union of the new heaven and new earth, the earth is 'heavenized.' The new earth is the focal site of the enthroned triune Presence, the center of a cosmic holy of holies (cf. Rev 11:19; 21:16)."[14]

We know that John's vision is highlighting not only the city like temple, but also the holy of holies, because the street of the city is "pure gold, like transparent glass" (Rev 21:21b). While our modern culture has retained the precious value of gold, we tend to think of it strictly in its monetary value or its aesthetic splendor. In

---

13 Cf. G. K. Beale, *The Temple and the Church's Mission: A Biblical Theology of the Dwelling Place of God*, NSBT (IVP, 2004): 253–56.

14 Meredith G. Kline, *God, Heaven and Har Magedon: A Covenantal Tale of Cosmos and Telos* (Wipf & Stock, 2006), 28.

2 Chr 3:8, however, the holy of holies is described as being overlaid "with six hundred talents of fine gold." That is approximately twenty-three tons of gold! But Solomon did not stop there; the whole of the was adorned in drapery made of gold.[15] For ancient Jews, the reference to streets of gold would conjure up images of the splendor of Solomon's temple, not least of which the holy of holies. Walking on gold was an entitlement of the high priest, who alone was permitted entry once a year into the most sacred space on earth. Therefore, for the city to be filled with streets of gold implies that citizens of the new Jerusalem are royal priests who are privileged to serve and worship God.

How exactly this will look in the life of the new creation is speculation this side of eternity. But what we can deduce from John's vision is a city as sacred as the holy of holies of the earthly temple. As golden cubes, the holy of holies and the new Jerusalem are clearly connected, the latter describing the fulfillment of the former. "God's special presence, formerly limited to the holy of holies, has now extended out to encompass the entire visible heavens and the whole earth, which the holy place and the court respectively symbolized."[16] And since the temple represented a microcosm of the whole universe, the descriptive imagery of the city in Rev 21 is transcendent, describing the condition of the entire new creation.

When my fiancée and I were engaged we lived many miles apart, I in Washington and my fiancée in San Diego. We utilized technology to talk on the phone every night. But now that we are married, it would be silly for me to call her on her cell phone every night. She is usually lying right next to me! Our nightly phone calls were necessary for that season apart, and they served as a temporary placeholder until we got to be fully present with each other. But now that we are together, there is no need for that anymore!

In light of this, why would we settle for God's veiled presence in the temple when we can forever be satisfied by God's manifest presence in the world to come? It is not that the new Jerusalem will lack a temple; instead, the entire world will be the temple, because

---

15 Cf. 1 Kgs 6:19–22, 28, 30; 7:48–50.
16 G. K. Beale, *A New Testament Biblical Theology: The Unfolding of the Old Testament in the New* (Baker Academic, 2011), 640.

our triune God will be the temple! No longer will you go to God's temple to worship. Everywhere will be sacred space, where every act is an act of worship. Enjoying God and enjoying God's new creation will be worship. "To live in this city is to live continually in the presence of the unveiled glory of God."[17]

City of Light

> And the city has no need of the sun or of the moon, that they shine on it, for the glory of God illuminates it, and its lamp is the Lamb. And the nations will walk by its light, and the kings of the earth will bring their glory into it. And its gates will never be shut by day (for there will be no night there), and they will bring the glory and the honor of the nations into it. And every unclean thing and one who practices detestable things and falsehood will never enter into it, except those who are written in the book of life of the Lamb. (Rev 21:23-27)

While it is possible that one may be unfamiliar with the name Vincent van Gogh, most have undoubtably encountered his famous painting *The Starry Night*. Van Gogh used a bright yellow in his paintings to symbolize the presence of God. In this particular painting, he filled the sky with big yellow circles, almost drawn in a spiral. However, there is something else that is fascinating about this painting. Van Gogh situated a church building in the village below, but no light comes from its windows. What one does notice is the light present in the homes of the village, showing that God's presence dwells in the community of people, not in an empty church building.

One could also conclude that God's creation, both in the physical universe and in His human creatures, reflects the divine light. Van Gogh's use of yellow light to demonstrate the divine is not wrong at all. The biblical imagery of light calls for a study all its own, but the concept is certainly applicable to these verses, as well.

---

[17] Bruce Milne, *The Message of Heaven and Hell: Grace and Destiny*, The Bible Speaks Today (InterVarsity Press, 2002), 317.

The Most Holy Place

In Rev 21:23-27 there appears to be a fulfillment of what had been promised back in Isa 60, specifically verses 1-3 and 19-20:

> Arise, shine! For your light has come, and the glory of Yahweh has risen on you. For look! darkness shall cover the earth, and thick darkness the peoples, but Yahweh will rise on you, and his glory will appear over you. And nations shall come to your light, and kings to the bright light of your sunrise.... The sun shall no longer be your light by day, and for bright light the moon shall not give you light, but Yahweh will be your everlasting light, and your God your glory. Your sun shall no longer go down, and your moon shall not wane, for Yahweh himself will be your everlasting light, and your days of mourning shall come to an end. (Isa 60:1-3, 19-20)

This Old Testament picture envisions God's glory eclipsing any glory we can find in the universe. As big as the sun is, *God is bigger.* As radiant as the sun is, *God is brighter.* As effective as the sun's rays are in altering us when we are exposed to them, exposure to God's glory is even more transformative.

Like the face of Moses glowing when he encountered the mere "back" side of God's glory, so also the concept of encountering God's glory implies that the recipient will be changed by the glory and then naturally reflect it outward.[18] *The new Jerusalem, being both a people and a place, is engulfed in the glory of God.*

His light, like a lamp with a bulb inside of it, will indwell us and illuminate us. We will indeed shine with a physical glory that will match our inner glorification. This seems fitting of biblical figures with heavenly bodies, since angels who appear to people did appear to be clothed in light (Acts 12:7; Luke 2:9). Moreover, as we have already discussed, our resurrection bodies are modeled after Christ's glorified body, and His body appears in majestic light, as when He confronted Paul on the Damascus road (Acts 9:3) and also in the book of Revelation (1:16; 21:23).

Similar to Isaiah, John's use of light in Revelation carries both physical and illustrative meaning. This is what makes apocalyptic

---

18 Exod 33:18-23 and 34:29-35. Cf. Smith, *Isaiah 40-66*, 626.

literature both difficult and exciting: Where does the symbolism end and the literalism begin? There is a sense in which God's glory does act as a luminary; however, it also acts as a transformative agent. This is not to say that the new creation will be devoid of stars, moons, etc. The apocalyptic imagery does not negate the existence of these things, but rather shows God's majesty superiority over these things. If these things will exist, they will be superfluous in comparison to the glory of God.

It is worth mentioning that in the ancient world, darkness was seen as a covering for all kinds of evil to take place. Saying that there will be an absence of night serves to articulate the point that evil will no longer have a covering because it will be fully exposed and done away with. Thus, the absence of the night is the absence of evil and danger. That is the message of their absence, more than any topographical notes.

Furthermore, the new Jerusalem has no need of a sun or a moon because "the glory of God illuminates it." Isaiah spoke of this coming day, when the Lord would be our "everlasting light," and when "our days of mourning shall come to an end" (60:19–20). Isaiah's oracle highlights the biblical theme of "light" being just as much about eschatological victory over the forces and effects of "darkness" as it is about literal radiance.

In the Johannine literature,[19] the usage of light conveys multiple things about God: His holy purity (1 John 1:5, 7), His salvation (1 John 1:8), and His glory (Rev 21:23). Believers are encouraged to "walk in the light" (1 John 1:5–7) since they belong to God, or to "the light." Jesus even declares Himself to be the "light of the world" (John 8:12). While there is much to be said about each of these verses, the important point for our discussion is to remember that light symbolizes the presence of God and His transformative power over the domain of darkness.

When studying the physics of light, it will become obvious just how pervasive light is. When darkness is met by light, darkness flees and the light conquers. John tells us that in Jesus is light (John 1:4). Christians embody the light of their Savior as they radiate

---

[19] Traditionally, the Johannine literature consists of the Gospel of John, 1–3 John, and Revelation.

and prevail over the surrounding darkness. John continues his emphasis on light, proclaiming, "light shines in the darkness, and the darkness did not overcome it" (1:5). Likewise, in Rev 22:16 Jesus is referred to as the "bright morning star" who secures victory over darkness. The cosmos after the eschaton will only have light. That, I believe, is the emphasis of this passage—not some absence of stars in the heavens, but the triumph of the light over the forces of darkness.

Why would the city need a wall if God's enemies have all been destroyed? Instead of preventing outsiders from coming in, the walls denote total security. The new world will not have to walls boxing believers in, thus restraining or protecting us from potential evil—evil will no presence in the new heavens and new earth. Instead, the walls are emblems of safety and the protection of God's providential care.

It is also important to note that John's apocalypse does not shy away from warnings of future judgment. Whenever hope is presented, on the heels of said hope is the looming promise of judgment. Because only light will pervade the new Jerusalem, those who walk in darkness will have no choice but to accept their fate of a life lived in outer darkness, banished outside the gates of the heavenly city. Their destruction will be their end. It is a sober warning to all readers to consider their current status and their need for a Savior.

Infinitely Happy in an Infinitely Happy God

The puritan John Whitlock once said, "This is the Christian's way and his end, his way is holiness, his end—happiness." I cannot reiterate the sheer happiness that should exude from every believer as we cherish the joy of our salvation and the coming of its full benefits. In his first letter, Peter presses this very point:

> Though you have not seen him, you love him. Though you do not now see him, you believe in him and rejoice with joy that is inexpressible and filled with glory, obtaining the outcome of your faith, the salvation of your souls. (1 Pet 1:8–9)

The inaugural benefit of our salvation stokes in us an "inexpressible" joy. It is unfortunate when Christians bemoan, "God does not want us to be happy; He wants us to be holy." such an utterance is misguided because it juxtaposes holiness and happiness as though they are inherently at odds with one another. However, this is not what the Bible portrays. In fact, the holiness is the way to happiness, and I hope this book has been in unpacking the idea that the coming new creation is one of both holiness and happiness.

Nevertheless, there is still more to unpack, more that should make our hearts leap with joy as we consider the grace of God. But do not just take my word for it. The following are thoughts from other believers about the intrinsic relationship between holiness and happiness.

Beginning with the "prince of preachers," Charles Spurgeon had this to say concerning John 15:11:

> A Christian has never fully realized what Christ came to make him until he has grasped the joy of the Lord. Christ wishes his people to be happy. When they are perfect, as he will make them in due time, they shall also be perfectly happy. As heaven is the place of pure holiness, so is it the place of unalloyed happiness; and in proportion as we get ready for heaven, we shall have some of the joy which belongs to heaven, and it is our Saviour's will that even now his joy should remain in us, and that our joy should be full.[20]

Again, Spurgeon on a different occasion, also avers:

> Many people seem to think that it is a very sorrowful thing to be a Christian, that believers in Christ are a miserable, unhappy lot of folk who never enjoy themselves.... *We serve a happy God*, and we believe in a joyous gospel, and the love of Christ in our hearts has made us anticipate many of the joys of heaven even while we are here on earth.[21]

---

20 C. H. Spurgeon, *The Metropolitan Tabernacle Pulpit Sermons*, vol. 51 (Passmore & Alabaster, 1905), 229.

21 Spurgeon, *The Metropolitan Tabernacle Pulpit Sermons*, 608, italics added

Considered for a moment the idea that God is a happy God? If we do not believe this truth about God, then we are training ourselves, and others, to believe that if we want holiness, we must go to God, but if we want happiness, we need to run the opposite direction. Do you see the danger in such a thought? We must believe that God is happy and the source of happiness, otherwise we will flee to wherever our heart finds it ultimate delight.

Spurgeon preached over five hundred times about the intimate relationship between holiness and happiness. For example, in one such incident he had this to say:

> One great part of the joy of the glorified will be the perfection of their characters, for he that is holy must be happy. Perfection of holiness must mean perfection of happiness, the two things must go together. Sin and sorrow cannot be divorced, and holiness and happiness cannot be separated.[22]

Be that as it may, I am not suggesting that we define happiness the same way the fallen world does. Our culture has definitions of love, peace, and happiness that are all much different from that of Scripture. Our definition of love is superficial at best; our peace is often times fragile and easily broken; and our happiness ebbs and flows with the tide of our emotions. But the joy of the Lord is not so! The Lord's type of joy is an indestructible joy.

Spurgeon also declared: "Believers are not dependent upon circumstances. Their joy comes not from what they have, but from what they are; not from where they are, but from whose they are."[23] We must never underestimate the quality of worship that comes from a happy heart.

Whether I am conscious of it or not, I glorify "The Taco Stand"[24] whenever I eat there. I enjoy every bite and I tell everyone I know that it is the best taco shop I have been to. Of course, I do not

---

for emphasis.

22 C. H. Spurgeon, *The Metropolitan Tabernacle Pulpit Sermons*, vol. 49 (Passmore & Alabaster, 1903), 19.

23 C. H. Spurgeon, *The Metropolitan Tabernacle Pulpit Sermons*, vol. 27 (Passmore & Alabaster, 1881), 77.

24 The name of the best taco shop in San Diego County, in my opinion.

worship tacos or any other food I enjoy. But I do worship God, and I recognize that any holy pleasure granted to me is, as Jonathan Edwards said, "only the stream. But God is the ocean." Any joy I receive should lead me to God, and in Him I can be totally immersed in divine happiness and dive into the infinite depths of His joy.

Jesus, in John 15:11, said, "I have spoken these things to you in order that my joy may be in you, and your joy may be made complete." This verse communicates Jesus's desire to give us the very joy that He Himself possesses and that He desires for our joy to be full. Not a "cup half full," but a cup full! Not full of fleeting joy, but full of the joy of the Lord, the very joy of Jesus!

But we must ask ourselves, Do we believe His words? We forget that one of the reasons Jesus came was to secure for us an indestructible joy. Furthermore, have we also forgotten that the fruit of the Spirit is joy (Gal 5:22–23)? That means that a natural byproduct of God's Spirit at work in our lives results in joy! Isaac Watts, the hymnwriter of the timeless "Joy to the World," said it best: "Religion was never designed to make our pleasures less."

The new creation will be a place of infinite, eternal happiness because of God's presence. The ancient context of God's presence being a "blessing" is literally God's presence "happifying" the recipients. Some have referred to heaven as "the happifying Presence of the glorious God."

So, when all of creation will be permeated with the presence of the triune God, then all of creation will be "happified" and all believers will be infinitely happy in the infinitely happy God. I close this section with a lengthy, but worthy quote by the puritan Stephen Charnock:

> The happiness depends upon the presence of God, with whom believers shall be for ever present. Happiness cannot perish as long as God lives.... The enjoyment of God will be as fresh and glorious after many ages as it was at first. God is eternal, and eternity knows no change; there will then be the fullest possession, without any decay in the object enjoyed. There can be nothing past, nothing future; time neither adds to it, nor detracts from it; that infinite fulness of perfection which

flourisheth in him now, will flourish eternally, without any discolouring of it in the least by those innumerable ages that shall run to eternity, much less any despoiling him of them.... He will have variety to increase delights, and eternity to perpetuate them; this will be the fruit of the enjoyment of an infinite, an eternal God. He is not a cistern, but a fountain, wherein water is always living, and never putrifies.[25]

Eden in Our Hearts

The high priest's breastplate found in Exod 28:15-20 was gold and embedded in it were twelve stones (twelve, think twelve tribes of Israel), each stone was different, but precious. The list of stones in Exod 28:15-20, Ezek 28:13, and Rev 21:18-20 is strikingly similar! Exodus says that the purpose of the high priest's breastplate would be to be a "memorial." What is it a memorial of? Eden, as evidenced by Ezek 28:13 where a strikingly similar list of stones was said to be found in Eden. What does this mean? Since Ezekiel suggests that these precious stones were found in Eden, and Revelation notes that these stones will be the foundation of the garden city of the new Jerusalem, the high priest's breastplate is therefore a symbol pointing *backwards and forwards* at the same time. It pointed *back* to Eden and *forward* to the new Jerusalem.

The precious stones on the high priest's shoulders served to remind the people of Eden of the ideal that should be kept alive in the hearts, dreams, and hopes of God's people. God intentionally put forth the high priest to be His representative for all Israel of the very life they lost but looked to regain, the paradise of Eden. The Lord encouraged his people with memorial stones of the past, pointing them towards their promised future. Therefore, as a royal priesthood (1 Pet 2:9; Rev 5:10) we are emblems of hope for a paradise regained.

As the high priest wore memorial stones of a paradise lost, so we, too, often long for what we have yet to experience. Did you catch that? Just like the high priest, we have long to return to a

---

[25] Stephen Charnock, *The Complete Works of Stephen Charnock*, vol. 1 (James Nisbet and Co., 1864-1866), 364-365.

place we have never been! It is paradoxical in a sense to understand that we will one day fulfill a desire we have always had the appetite for, but never had the luxury to taste for ourselves. The paradox lies in that we will taste life as it always was meant to be, but as we never previously had it. Even Adam and Eve never experienced anything as good as the new creation will be! We were designed to have a longing for the new world. We hold the ideal of Eden in our hearts.

8

The World Created for the Son

> *The first Eden was made for Adam and his bride; the final Eden is going to be made for Christ and His bride.*

AFTER NEARLY A DECADE of preparations, in 2009 James Cameron released his cinematic masterpiece. Avatar captured audiences' imagination not with its storyline or acting, but by the stunning beauty of otherworldly Pandora. I remember sitting in the theater enthralled, as my eyes saw what my mind had always pictured the world should look like. It was the lush vegetation, the vibrant colors like neon highlighters, the flowing streams of water and waterfalls, and the harmony in which the creatures dwelled among the creation. It all seemed like a dance, glorifying the creator of such a place as Pandora.

As the movie progressed, the plot and the characters faded, and my mind ran wild, imagining what life might be like in Pandora. Over the years, I have not forgotten how I felt when I first saw that movie, and it has ignited my imagination even more so ever since.

However, my imagination is not fixated on some far-off fantasy that will never come to fruition. On the contrary, my imagination is fixated on the promised new world that God will create and in which He will dwell fully, as promised throughout the Bible. Even the beauty of James Cameron's Pandora does not hold a candle to the awe of the new world promised in Scripture. But have we been awakened to it?

Paradoxically Nostalgic and New

> And he showed me the river of the water of life, bright as crystal, flowing out from the throne of God and of the Lamb in the middle of the street of the city, and on both sides of the river is the tree of life, producing twelve fruits, yielding its fruit according to every month, and the leaves of the tree are for the healing of the nations. (Rev 22:1–2, my translation)

It is clear in the closing chapters of Revelation that John intends for us to read Rev 21–22 in the light of Gen 1–2, and as we do, we should also feel a sense of biblical nostalgia. Genesis begins with the *first* Eden, and Revelation ends with the *last* Eden. The nostalgia is paradoxical, because with as much as we feel a sense of longing for something from the far distant past, it is also something totally new.

Or, to put it another way, the *continuity* of the new creation coexists alongside a very real sense of *discontinuity* as well. While the new creation will user in an existence previously unknown throughout the cosmos, there is also a very real sense of familiarity with the world made new. And that is how Revelation often reads. John struggles to find the right words to communicate in words the imagery of his visions, even under the influence of the Holy Spirit.

To simply say that Eden has been restored is not to do justice to what the Scriptures say. For example, the first Eden lacked the throne of God and the Lamb. God ruled from heaven above, but now He dwells with His people on earth. Eden has been elevated and expanded for the glory of God and for the enjoyment of His people throughout all eternity.

The Life-Giving Garden

Talk to any number of people and you will quickly find that many are unsatisfied with the world the way it is. Even the most content of souls, if they are honest, will admit that their desires are weighty and that the lives they currently live cannot fully satiate the longings of their heart.

It is no accident that we feel the way we do. I have never met someone who would say this world matches up with all of their ideals. And if we are honest, this world is far worse than we even admit. Not only this world, but we, individually, are both the victims and the culprits of such depravity.

In high school, I was a wrestler. This required supreme conditioning and discipline. There were some practices when I would be so thirsty that nothing else was on my mind. Finishing the drill to obtain a drink of water was all that mattered. All of us have an unquenchable thirst for a drink of something we have never yet tasted.

In John 4, Jesus spoke to a woman at a well, in metaphorical language, about eternal life, alluding to it as "water." He then declared to this woman, "Whoever drinks of this water which I will give to him will never be thirsty for eternity, but the water which I will give to him will become in him a well of water springing up to eternal life" (John 4:14). Jesus contrasts natural solutions for solving our deepest needs with supernatural solutions. Those who drink natural water thirst again and eventually die. In stark contrast, those who drink "living water" are satisfied and obtain eternal life.

The solution to our needs and desires is not within us, as much as our culture promises this to be the case. The solution is outside of us and inside the Jesus—the very one who invites us to drink and find life. Because we are God's image bearers, only He can satisfy our deepest desire. The English Puritan, John Flavel, insightfully wrote: "[Christ] is bread to the hungry, water to the thirsty, a garment to the naked, healing to the wounded; and whatever a soul can desire is found in him."[1] Revelation 22:17 invites the "one who is thirsty" to drink the "water of life freely." This reminds us, yet again, that all of God's eschatological blessings are received by grace.

The opening verses of Revelation 22 reveal a life-giving garden that will undo the effects of sin in the present life. The same angel who showed John the vision of the new Jerusalem now unveils a

---

1 John Flavel, *The Whole Works of the Reverend John Flavel*, vol. 2 (London; Edinburgh; Dublin: W. Baynes and Son; Waugh and Innes; M. Keene, 1820), 216.

vision of the new Eden—the place where our God-given thirst can be quenched.

Two main elements in the Edenic garden demand careful attention: "the river of the water of life" and "the tree of life." Both are life-giving elements given by God and to promote an environment of vibrant, unending existence.

The "river of the water of life" is reminiscent of the rivers in Eden and Ezek 47:1–12. At its core, the river is a symbol of eternal life. But within this broad meaning, we find more specific illustrations of its symbolism. Psalm 36 speaks of the loyal love of God and the blessing of knowing Him: "You feed them from the abundance of your own house, letting them drink from your river of delights. For you are the fountain of life, the light by which we see" (Ps 36:8–9 NLT).

The word translated as "delights" is a fascinating word. In Hebrew it is the plural form of Eden, and certainly this psalm highlights the joy of the future by looking back at Eden before the fall. Psalm 36 recognizes, as does the book of Revelation, that while Eden was home to rivers of life, God is the fountain of life.

While the river of Rev 22 has rich symbolism, this does not negate the idea that the new creation will have lush flowing rivers, perhaps even mystic in both appearance and effect. The word "bright" is the Greek word *lampros*, the same word used to describe Jesus as the "bright morning star" (Rev 22:16) and the angels clothed in "bright linen" (15:6). Jesus even said that the righteous would "shine like the sun in the kingdom" (Matt 13:43).

Therefore, since we already noted above that everything in the new creation appears to radiate light and beauty, it would not be a stretch to understand the adjectival phrase "bright as crystal" as possessing some type of illuminating characteristics.[2] What Rev 22 reveals about the river of the water of life indicates for the readers how end will not merely be a *restoration* of the Eden, "but will be

---

2 The CEB translates this description as "shining like crystal," whereas the GNT translates it as "sparkling like crystal." Again, I imagine the luminescent rivers and vegetation of Pandora from James Cameron's *Avatar* to be the closest thing I can think of to the type of beauty and radiance that is described in Revelation 21–22. Nevertheless, such cinematic beauty pales in comparison to the splendor and majesty of all God has prepared for His people (cf. 1 Cor 2:9).

something new in which God consummates with unrestricted fullness the works and ways begun at creation."³

One further element in this garden-city is the tree of life, which may be foreign to many modern readers, but was very familiar to the ancient audience. In His letters to the churches, Jesus motivates believers with eschatological rewards that will be theirs to receive if they can endure in the faith. While these rewards are for every all believers, the language of the rewards are contextualized to speak to each city (see below under the subsection *The Tree of Life*). In the letter to the church in Ephesus (Rev 2:1-7), Jesus promises that the one who prevails will be able to eat from the tree of life, something even Adam and Eve never got to do. This is the promise of immortality.

The Tree of Life

One of the recipients of the letter of Revelation, Ephesus was an important city in the history of the early Church. John, who penned Revelation, was familiar with the city of Ephesus and knew they would understand the tree of life motif communicated to them in Rev 2:7.

Ephesus was a vibrant city in the Roman Empire. The city attracted worshipers from all parts of the empire, which in turn stimulated its economy. Without a doubt the biggest draw to the city was its magnificent temple dedicated to the worship of the goddess Artemis, the goddess of fertility (cf. Acts 19:27, 35).

Excavations and historical sources have unearthed significant insights into this ancient city. It has become clear that the magnificent Temple of Artemis was accompanied by a robust garden. In the center of the garden was a tree shrine, most likely that of an oak or an elm tree. The evidence leans to support that the "tree shrine" was the most sacred part of the temple and could very well have been spoken of as the "tree of life."

"Worship of Artemis was certainly the most popular of the

---

3 Karl Heinrich Rengstorf, "Ποταμός, Ποταμοφόρητος, Ἰορδάνης," edited by Gerhard Kittel, Geoffrey W. Bromiley, and Gerhard Friedrich. *TDNT* (Grand Rapids, MI: Eerdmans, 1964-76), 6:604-605.

Ephesian cults and was an important figure of civic pride." To her was ascribed "unsurpassed cosmic power," including the power to raise people from the dead.[4] Why was this reward chosen for the Ephesians? Perhaps it is to contrast what paganism promised: access to the tree of life, which only Christianity could rightfully deliver.

Jewish apocalyptic literature was anything but silent about the expectancy of the tree of life reappearing in a radically renovated world. Consider the following three passages from Second Temple Jewish literature:

> Because it is for you that paradise is opened, the tree of life is planted, the age to come is prepared, plenty is provided, a city is built, rest is appointed, goodness is established and wisdom perfected beforehand. The root of evil is sealed up from you, illness is banished from you, and death is hidden; Hades has fled and corruption has been forgotten; sorrows have passed away, and in the end the treasure of immortality is made manifest. (2 Esd 8:52–54 NRSV)

> And he shall open the gates of paradise, and shall remove the threatening sword against Adam. And he shall give to the saints to eat from the tree of life, and the spirit of holiness shall be on them. (*T. Levi* 18:10–11)[5]

> And as for this sweet-smelling tree [the tree of life], no flesh has power to touch it until the great decision, in which there is vengeance for all and a completion forever. Then its fruit will be given to the just and holy chosen ones for life and for food; and it will be transplanted to the holy place from the house of God, King of the age. (*1 En.* 25:4 LES)

Clearly, Jewish expectation reveals that the tree is a symbol of

---

4 Craig A. Evans and Craig A. Bubeck, editor, *John's Gospel, Hebrews–Revelation*, The Bible Knowledge Background Commentary (Colorado Springs, CO; Paris, ON; Eastbourne: David C Cook, 2005), 355–356.

5 Robert Henry Charles, editor, *Pseudepigrapha of the Old Testament,* vol. 2 (Clarendon Press, 1913), 315.

eschatological life and immortality given to the righteous.

The "tree of life" even finds its way into two more verses before the close of the letter—Rev 22:14 and 18; verse 14 says, "Blessed are the ones who wash their robes, so that their authority will be over the tree of life and they may enter into the city through the gates." Inheriting the tree of life is synonymous with inheriting immortality. Greater than the fountain of youth, the tree of life is an explicit symbol of the abolition of death, the curse of sin being lifted, and the anticipation of immortality realized by those who partake of its fruit.

Returning again to Rev 22, we notice the tree of life is on both sides of the river. It is possible that this is a grove of trees that give life. These trees produce "twelve fruits, yielding its fruit according to every month" (22:2), indicating both the diverse variety and the accessible availability of the blessed fruit.

The original audience knew all too well the reality of feast and famine. Greco-Roman society was built on agriculture system and dependent upon it for sustaining life. Therefore, the very idea of a life-sustaining tree producing fruit on a monthly basis would be an invaluable commodity to any family farm. Furthermore, if the fruit of our earthly trees provide sweet relief from the pangs of hunger, how much more will the fruit of the heavenly tree of life satisfy our hunger for eternal life!

Notice also that the leaves provide "healing for the nations" embody the fulfillment of Ezek 47:12. But this begs the question: What need is there for healing foliage in a world devoid of death and sickness? I propose that what needs healing are the emotional wounds of the present life. How wonderful it is to think that the emotional scars we have will find a bliss that can undo even the worst of our sufferings.

While the original Eden was "very good," the eschatological Eden is perfect, in every sense of the word. Beale writes, "Both Ezekiel 47 and Revelation 22:1–2 picture a recapitulation of the original garden of Eden, though in an even more escalated fertile form."[6] The flourishing conditions and lush nature make the first Eden dry in comparison.

---

6 G. K. Beale, *A New Testament Biblical Theology: The Unfolding of the Old*

Elements like the river of the water of life, bright as crystal, far surpass the river of Eden. The tree of life on both sides, creating groves of trees, trumps the single tree of the first garden. This is a life-giving garden, whose symbolism is matched only by its vibrant, colorful elegance.

Further Old Testament passages help paint the picture for us. Joel 3:18 speaks of "mountains" that will "drip new wine." Amos elaborates on this, noting that "the hills will flow with" this sweet wine. Such language is symbolic of feast and festivity, abundance and euphoria.

Not only will our needs be provided for, but luxurious blessings such as wine will be "flowing" in the mountain and the hills. Even animals will live in abundance and peace, without the need to hunt or threaten the harmony of our existence by posing a danger to us. "They will not destroy" anyone or anything (cf. Isa 11:6–9). There will be plenty for all, and there will be harmony in the new creation.

The depiction of the new creation in Rev 21:1–22:5 suggests a unique blend of elements of architecture and nature. It is without questions a beautiful description of a "garden-city." Perhaps the closest earthly example of such a city is found in Singapore, where the whole city consists of an expanding garden. Giant man-made structures have been built with imports of nature. Trees, flowers, and other parts that form an ecosystem are cultivated on the outside and inside of many buildings. Thanks to this new ecosystem, there has been a return of some wildlife to the city, encouraging people everywhere that there is a possibility for humanity's habitation to blend well with animals of all sorts. The architects of the city have revealed that they truly believe humanity has an innate desire to live among nature.

Our advances in technology do not presuppose a depreciation of nature or threat its existence. Singapore highlights not only a foreshadowing of the garden-city described, but it also presents a reality where humanity acts as caretakers of the original creation. While ecologists often fret over the future of earth, it is encouraging to remind ourselves that God will someday make a glorious

---

Testament in the New (Grand Rapids: Baker Academic, 2011), 935.

new earth free from the current ecological problems that plague the place we call home.

Be that as it may, the promise of a new creation does not relieve humanity of its responsibility as stewards of Earth and the ecological problems that persist. On the contrary, humanity is obligated to work for solutions to these problems, not with a feeling of despair, but in the confidence of God's promised new creation. It is in light of this responsibility that I wholeheartedly recommend Sandra L. Richter's book *Stewards of Eden: What Scripture Says about the Environment and Why it Matters*.[7] In Richter's excellent study you will find discussions on the theology of creation, reasons for creation care, practical examples of what is wrong and what we can do about it. Again, if we care to preach the good news of the gospel and the hope of a resurrected cosmos, we must also be ready to treat the material world different *even now*.

Looking into the Eyes of the Creator

> And every curse will be no more, and the throne of God and of the Lamb will be in it, and His servants will serve Him, and they will see His face for themselves, and His name will be on their foreheads. (Rev 22:3–4, author translation)

These two verses encapsulate some of the most satisfying language in all of Scripture. Revelation 22:3 is reiterating that the garden of God will be life-giving and that all of creation will be void of "every curse."

Curse language is inextricably tied to the ramifications resulting from the fall (cf. Gen 3) and describes that which is unacceptable to God. The lifting of the curse means that the presence and the effects of sin will be no more. Death and decay are unacceptable to God and foreign to the life of heaven.

This fulfills the promise to the churches in Rev 2:11, in which the overcomer is promised to "never be harmed by the second death." In Isaiah's last vision of the new creation (Isa 66:22–24),

---

[7] Sandra L. Richter, *Stewards of Eden: What Scripture Says About the Environment and Why it Matters* (IVP Academic, 2020).

Isaiah prophesies about the everlasting life that is to be anticipated, lasting forever, "from new moon to new moon." He concludes his vision with a graphic warning to, suggesting that the people of God will "go out and look at the corpses of the people who have rebelled against" God (Isa 66:24a).

The first death was destructive, but God's mercy allowed redemption through Christ. The second death is permanent. Those who face the second death will not be given life again; they are destroyed, never able to destroy God's good creation again. Anthony Hoekema articulately notes:

> The total work of Christ is nothing less than to redeem this entire creation from the effects of sin. That purpose will not be accomplished until God has ushered in the new earth, until Paradise Lost has become Paradise Regained. We need a clear understanding of the doctrine of the new earth, therefore, in order to see God's redemptive program in cosmic dimensions. We need to realize that God will not be satisfied until the entire universe has been purged of all the results of man's fall.[8]

Now that God's dwelling place resides on a new earth, so too is "the throne of God and of the Lamb" present in the garden city. The Greek verb *latreuō* in Rev 22:3, translated as "serve," carries the idea of service through worship. It denotes the meaning "to serve as priest."[9] Serving God in this priestly denotes a sense worshipful relationship. Therefore, in response to God creating us for Himself, revealing Himself to us, and being steadfast in His love towards us our response is one of adoration and worship, declaring God as the supreme object of our affection. This is what it means to serve God—to adore Him and live obedient lives in response to all He has first done for us.

Such a ministry of worshipful service is exclusively offered to God in both the Old and New Testaments, with God's people

---

8 Anthony A. Hoekema, *The Bible and the Future* (Grand Rapids: Eerdmans), 275.

9 Robert G. Bratcher and Howard Hatton, *A Handbook on the Revelation to John*, UBS Handbook Series (New York: United Bible Societies, 1993), 313.

functioning as priest service to Him. For example, Isaiah notes that in the future believers "shall be called the priests of the; they shall speak of you as the ministers of our God" (Isa 61:6; cf. 66:21). In the New Testament we find a similar theme in the first letter of Peter: "But you are ... a royal priesthood (1 Pet 2:9). It seems clear from both the Old and New Testament that the people of God are considered a royal priesthood both now and in the new heavens and earth.

There is a potential issue with respect to the object of devotion in 22:3-4. At the end of 22:3 we note that believers "will serve *him*." This brings up the question of who is the recipient of said service: God or the Lamb? The question again remains open-ended in 22:4, where we read believers "will see *his*, and *his* name will be on their foreheads." To whom are the pronouns "him/his" referring to? God? Or the Lamb? The best answer is both.[10]

The singular "Him" indicates the unity of the Father and the Son in receiving worship, which is not surprising considering the numerous instances for unity throughout Revelation between the two distinct persons of the single divine essence. The following chart helps to illustrate this unity:

The Father	The Son
Hair like white wool (Dan 7:9)	Hair like white wool (Rev 1:14)
King of kings and Lord of lords (1 Tim 6:15; cf. Deut 10:17)	King of kings and Lord of lords (Rev 17:14; 19:16; cf. Acts 17:17)
*The First and the Last (Isa 41:4; 44:6; 48:12, Note that it is Yahweh, the Lord, speaking in these)	The First and the Last (Rev 1:17; 2:8)
The Alpha and Omega (Rev 21:6)	The Alpha and Omega (Rev 22:13; Rev 1:8)
Worshiped as deity (Rev 4:8-11)	Worshiped as deity (Rev 5:8-12)
Worshiped with [Jesus] the Lamb (Rev 5:13-14)	Worshiped with the one on the throne (Rev 5:13-14)

---

10 Cf. G. K. Beale, *The Book of Revelation: A Commentary on the Greek Text*, NIGTC (Grand Rapids; Carlisle, Cumbria: W. B. Eerdmans; Paternoster Press, 1999), 1114.

Conclusion: The Father shares in the same essence of deity as the Son, while being distinct in person and role. Both are co-equal and co-eternal.	*Conclusion*: The Son shares in the same essence of deity as the Father, while being distinct in person and role. Both are co-equal and co-eternal.

Turning to Rev 22:4, we now encounter perhaps the most glorious phrase in all of Revelation: "And they will see His face for themselves, and His name will be on their foreheads." To fully understand the magnitude of this passage it is important to first unpack a few aspects of biblical theology that are related to the idea of seeing God face to face.

In Exod 33:18–23, Moses is pleading with God to show him His glory (33:18). God's response to Moses is profound:

> And he said, "I myself will cause all my goodness to pass over before you, and I will proclaim the name of Yahweh before you, and I will be gracious to whom I will be gracious, and I will show compassion to whom I will show compassion." But he said, "You are not able to see my face, because a human will not see me and live." And Yahweh said, "There is a place with me, and you will stand on the rock. And when my glory passes over, I will put you in the rock's crevice, and I will cover you with my hand until I pass over. And I will remove my hand, and you will see my back, but my face will not be visible." (Exod 33:19–23)

These five verses are saturated in a biblical theology of God's glory. In these verses we discover something significant about God's nature—God's face cannot be seen by sinful humanity, even one like Moses, who would speak to God as one speaks to his friends (cf. Exod 33:9–11). At the heart of humanity is an innate desire to see God face to face, the very one whose image we are hand-crafted in the likeness of. This stems from the ancient belief that to see God's face means to know Him as He actually is. Richard Bauckham highlights this very thing, positing that "[t]he face expresses who a person is. To see God's face will be to know who God is in his personal being. This will be the heart of humanity's eternal joy in their eternal worship of God."[11] It was considered the pinnacle of blessing to have God's face shine upon you (cf. Num 6:25).[12] And so it became part of Jewish liturgy to exhort one another to seek the face of God (e.g., Pss 24:6; 27:8; 105:4).

As eschatology developed alongside the canon of Scripture, it became clear that seeing the face of God was the highest hope for the righteous and the means of their greatest satisfaction. Take, for example, the words of the psalmist: "Because I am righteous, I will see you. When I awake, I will see you face to face and be satisfied" (Ps 17:15 NLT).[13] Likewise, Jesus affirmed this expectation in the Beatitudes, stating, "Blessed are the pure in heart, because they will see God" (Matt 5:8).

Revelation 21–22 has been a constant unraveling of language that presents the fact that God's presence is more intimate than we could have imagined. It starts off broad, but beautiful, with God making His home with us (Rev 21:1–8). Then we discover that the heavenly city will be a cosmic holy of holies (Rev 21:9–27), where God's presence was a privilege exclusively experienced by the high priest. Finally, there is the highest form of divine intimacy granted to us, as God does not stop at making His home with us or gracing us with His presence, but actually shows us His face (Rev 22:4), something never afforded to humanity before.

"They will see His face for themselves." But whose face, exactly, shall we see? God the Father? God the Son? Again, as was the case in Rev 22:3, the answer is both.[14] To stare upon the Creator of the

---

11 Richard Bauckham, *The Theology of the Book of Revelation* (Cambridge: Cambridge University Press, 1993), 142.

12 Walter A. Elwell and Barry J. Beitzel, "Presence of God," *Baker Encyclopedia of the Bible* (Baker Book House, 1988), 1751.

13 Second Esdras 7:98 infers that the righteous will see the face of God after their death.

14 The personal pronoun referring to both the Father and the Son is a sort of poetic ambiguity used in Revelation to show the "oneness" (cf. John 10:30) of the two persons. This is another example of God's complex unity as described in the trinity. For example, the latter part of Rev 11:15 says, "The kingdom of the world has become the kingdom of our Lord and of his Christ, and he will reign forever and ever." Notice the pronoun "he" at the end is a singular pronoun, but

cosmos and gaze upon His beauty is a privilege only the redeemed will experience.

Scripture informs us that "whenever he is revealed we will be like him, because we will see him just as he is" (1 John 3:2). This encourages us that being face to face with God (as 1 Cor 13:12 anticipates) will be a transformative experience, one in which our sanctification will be instantly complete and "we will be like him" (cf. Rom 8:29–30; 1 Cor 15:49; Col 3:10).

But how can this be? How can gazing upon the face of God effect such a radical transformation? I know this can be true, even from an experience I have had on this side of life. As a husband, I remember as my bride made her way down the aisle to meet me. She was the most beautiful bride imaginable, and to my eyes it was as if no one else was present in the room. In that moment, nothing else and no one else could have lured my attention away from her.

In a far more glorious way, we will one day gaze upon the source and quintessence of beauty. And on that day, nothing else will ever take our gaze off of the one who has redeemed us from our sin. This is to the climax of our happiness; the satisfaction of our souls; the heaven of heaven—to see the face of God. We will see the face of the Creator of the cosmos and all our sorrow and pain will melt away in the fires of universal redemption.

Some have asked, "How do we know there will be no sorrow or pain in heaven?" We know this because there will be nothing that is able to pull us away from the unveiled beauty of God. The life we will live in eternity will not permit us to wonder about if there may be something better. This is because we "shall literally and physically, with [our] risen bodies, actually look into the face of Jesus."[15] Our new, resurrected, imperishable bodies will be such that we shall be able to behold the face of God in its full glory. As

---

its antecedent is both the "Lord" and "Christ." I believe the grammar is intentional and suggests that both the Lord and Christ will reign.

15 C. H. Spurgeon, "The Heaven of Heaven," in *The Metropolitan Tabernacle Pulpit Sermons*, vol. 14 (Passmore & Alabaster, 1868), 437. Spurgeon continues, "And this involves a fifth privilege, namely, complete transformation. 'They shall be like him, for they shall see him as he is.' If they see his face they shall be 'changed from glory to glory' by this face-to-face vision of the Lord. Beholding Christ, his likeness is photographed upon them; they become in all respects like

Paul puts it, "now we see through a mirror indirectly, but then face to face" (1 Cor 13:12).

This face-to-face relationship with God includes one further element, namely that the name of God will be on the foreheads of His people (Rev 22:4). To have the name of God on the forehead is a sign of protection, belonging, and closeness of relationship. In the Old Testament, the high priest wore the sacred name of God on his forehead when he entered the holy of holies, the very place of God's presence on earth. The golden plate that the high priest wore on his head was engraved with the words: "Holy to Yahweh" (cf. Exod 28:36–38). This allusion intensifies the notion that all believers will have the priestly privilege of intimate nearness to God.

In the book of Revelation the name on the forehead exposes one's allegiance and belonging. What we find in Revelation are two options: one is either marked by God, as is in Rev 22:4, or by the beast, referred to by John as the infamous "mark of the beast" (cf. Rev 14:9; 17:5; 20:4. Those marked on their forehead by God are sealed and protected from God's impending wrath (cf. Rev 7:3; 9:4). Those who take the mark of the beast fall under the wrath of God.

The presence of God's name on the foreheads of His people fulfills the promise to the overcomer. In Rev 3:12 Jesus promised to "write on him the name of my God and the name of the city of my God, the new Jerusalem that comes down from heaven from my God, and my new name." The name of God written on the Christian highlights his belonging to God and marks out him to receive His love and affection.

Osborne provides a helpful insight into the importance of God's and its application for believers:

> Not only will they have a permanent home but also a new name written on them.... It is "the name of my God," fitting the adoption imagery of Romans 8:15 (by the Spirit we cry "Abba Father!") and signifying that we partake of his essence

---

him as they gaze upon him [in a] world without end" (Spurgeon, "Heaven of Heaven," 492).

as his children. There is also probably an echo of Isaiah 62:2, the "new name bestowed" by Yahweh on faithful Israel.[16]

The name of the city that is embossed upon the Christian symbolizes authentic citizenship in the coming heavenly city. and their rightful ownership of this future city. Like a parking space reserved exclusively for an important person, the new Jerusalem is a city exclusively enjoyed by those who are marked by God and have the name of the city engraved upon them.

Lastly, while the presence of Christ's "new name" is somewhat ambiguous, it nevertheless indicates a special relationship between Christ and His people. Because biblical imagery points to union with Christ as a picture of marriage, the act of Christ writing His name on His people symbolizes how in modern American culture the wife takes on the husband's last name, thus inheriting all that he has and all that he is.

In a similar fashion, Christ loves His bride with all that He is and gives her all that He has. And because Christ has a "name above every name" (Phil 2:9), we can trust that there is nothing outside of His royal rule that would ever threaten us.

The Kingdom of the Son

> And night will be no more, and they will have no need of the light of a lamp and the light of the sun, because the Lord God will shine on them, and they will reign forever into eternity. (Rev 22:5, author's translation)

The reign of the triune God is not something we passively will observe. Astonishingly, God will entrust His redeemed people to reign with Him. In the ultimate turn of events, the one who was formerly estranged from God now, by God's transformational power, is a saint reigning with Christ the King. Human hierarchy has no place in the coming kingdom because the Lord will be King and we will be individually equal, participating in the collective whole as we

---

16 Grant R. Osborne, *Revelation: Verse by Verse*, Osborne New Testament Commentaries (Bellingham: Lexham Press, 2016), 80.

live out the responsibility of kingship with the King over the new creation. As Brooks notes, "[w]e shall share in Christ's royalty and we shall live like kings. And we shall be like this for ever and ever!"[17]

While Rev 22:3 refers to believers as priests participating in worshipful service, Rev 22:5 highlights the kingship of believers over the new creation. The prophet Daniel prophesied that God's people would "receive the kingdom" and possess it "forever and ever" (Dan 7:18). It is the fulfillment of this prophecy that we see in Rev 22:5.

The crowns given to believers (Rev 2:10; 3:11) will be put to use as we are given royal responsibilities as members of the family of God forever. What was sung about in hopeful expectation (5:10) will now be a cosmic reality.

As a wedding is a celebration of a new beginning, so the end of history is the new beginning of life itself. Everything will be new. As Jonathan Edwards poignantly remarks: "The end of God's creating the world, was to prepare a kingdom for his Son, (for he is appointed heir of the world,) which should remain to all eternity."[18]

An excerpt from the Dead Sea Scrolls not only affirms that the new earth will become like Eden, but that it will be ruled by a son: "All the world will be like Eden, and all ... the earth will be at peace forever, and ... a beloved son ... will ... inherit it all" (4Q475, 5–7). Therefore, it has been destined since before the first creation that the Son of God would be the rightful owner of the new creation.

This is what Paul alludes to in Col 1:13, when believers are said to be "transferred" to the "kingdom of the Son." In the same vein, Heb 1:8 applies Ps 45:6 to the Son: "Your throne, O God, is forever and ever, and the scepter of righteous is the scepter of your kingdom." Thus, it is a joint "kingdom of Christ and God" (Eph 5:5; cf. Rev 11:15).

However, the primary reason Jesus is revealed to humanity as the "Son of God" is to proclaim His functional role as heaven's Prince, who in His incarnation redeemed the world and became

---

17 Richard Brooks, *The Lamb Is All the Glory* (Welwyn Commentary Series. Darlington, England: Evangelical Press, 1986), 195.

18 Jonathan Edwards, *The Works of Jonathan Edwards*, vol. 1 (Banner of Truth Trust, 1974), 584.

King of all the new creation. But what king reigns without his bride? The King of kings has chosen His bride and marks her with His name (Rev 3:12; 22:4); He then rules with her forever (22:5).

We have alluded to the marital language in Revelation throughout this book. Such language takes us back to the Old Testament, in which the Lord claims to be a spouse to His people. This motif of marriage is found throughout the Bible. Isaiah 54:5 makes a strong appeal that the Lord ("your Maker") is the spouse of His people. It is difficult to miss this theme, but it is also challenging to deal with such a robust reality in a concise manner.

Perhaps the most well-known Old Testament passage that refers to God and His bride is found in the book of Hosea. In Hos 2 we read: "And I [the Lord] will betroth you to me forever. I will betroth you to me in righteousness and in justice, in steadfast love and in mercy. I will betroth you to me in faithfulness. And you shall know the Lord" (2:19–20 ESV). The New Testament picks up this theme and further build upon it. In Eph 5:32 Paul relates the following to the church in Ephesus: "This mystery is great, but I am speaking with reference to Christ and the church." Paul calls human marriage, which is the first marriage, a signpost pointing to the final marriage between Christ and the Church.

All other metaphors in the Bible are using the substance to relate to the shadow. For example, Christ and the Church are like vines and branches (cf. John 15), using an already existing and natural element for analogous purposes. But none are like the metaphor of marriage, in which the man and the woman are the prototype and the metaphor but not the final form of marriage. Christ and the Church are the reality. Men and women are the shadow, but Christ and the Church are the substance of marriage. The first Eden was made for Adam and his bride; the final Eden will be made for the second Adam and His Bride.[19] The puritan Thomas Goodwin concurs:

> As Adam had a world made for him, so shall Jesus Christ, this second Adam—Adam being a type of him that was to

---

19 The theme of Christ being the last Adam can be found most explicitly in Rom 5 and 1 Cor 15.

come—have a world made for him. This world was not good enough for him; he hath a better appointed than that which old Adam had, a new heaven and a new earth, according to the promise, Isaiah 66:22, where the saints shall reign.[20]

Jesus Is So Much More

Too often I have heard people remark: "if we were perfect, we would have no need for Jesus." I cannot recall how many times I have cringed upon hearing fellow believers use this. To adhere to this phrase is to admit that if perfection were possible there would be no need for a relationship with Christ. Before moving forward, it is important to challenge the meaning of perfection in this familiar saying. If perfection is determined by moral finality and ethical purity, are we not then working with an incomplete definition?

As I mentioned in the opening chapter of this book, sinless is not the equivalent of perfection. If this were so, Adam and Eve would have lived in perfection. It is worth reiterating that Adam and Eve did not experience the highest form of life. Yes, it was far superior to humanity's current experience, but it was also far inferior to the life to come at the eschaton.

The aforementioned phrase implies that Christianity should be twisted into what we can gain from our Savior, like a leech sucking the life out of its host. We do not come Christ as to a drinking fountain, to gain sustenance and depart until we are thirsty once more. Jesus is much more than the paschal lamb who takes away our sins and he demands our utmost devotion to Him.

Rather, salvation commences when Jesus satisfies our supreme need; and salvation culminates when Jesus satisfies our infinite desire. In saying this we note that Jesus is not only the source of eternal life, He is the *telos*, the very apex of all of God's promises.

Of all the pleasures that await us in the new creation, none can eclipse the reciprocal love and happiness to be found in Christ. To "see His face" is to see His unveiled glory. The beauty that would blind us in our current physical bodies will be visible in our

---

20 Thomas Goodwin, *The Works of Thomas Goodwin*, vol. 1 (James Nichol, 1861), 510.

resurrection bodies. We will behold the King in His beauty and our "eyes will see the king in his beauty" (Isa 33:17).

To see the face of God will be the heaven of heaven. We will truly discover, if we are not convinced already, that Jesus not only has satisfied our greatest need, but that He will forever and ever satisfy us. We will continue to indulge in that satisfaction in the new creation, where time is irrelevant, and bliss is boundless. Endless adventure awaits us, and I express my excitement by inviting anyone and everyone to know the God who is the author of such everlasting delight in a resurrected cosmos.

9

Conclusion

The End Is the New Beginning

> *The life of a Christian is wondrously ruled in this world by the consideration and meditation of the life of another world.*[1]
> —Richard Sibbes

THE FINAL BOOK OF C. S. Lewis's *Chronicles of Narnia, The Last Battle*, has an immense focus on death. It is almost as if Lewis wanted to encourage the reader to rethink death from a biblical worldview.

There is one scene, in particular, worth spending some time discussing. In this scene, Aslan converses with the children who have been with him throughout their journeys and who up until this moment in the story had not fully realized their fate. It is at with these words that Aslan gently breaks the news to them:

> "There was a real railway accident," said Aslan softly. "Your father and mother and all of you are—as you used to call it in the Shadowlands—dead. The term is over: the holidays have begun. The dream is ended: this is morning."
>
> And as He spoke He no longer looked to them like a lion; but the things that began to happen after that were so great and beautiful that I cannot write them. And for us this is the end of all the stories, and we can most truly say that they all lived

---

1 Richard Sibbes, "A Glance of Heaven" in *The Complete Works of Richard Sibbes*, vol. 4, edited by Alexander Balloch Grosart (Edinburgh: James Nichol, 1863), 170.

happily ever after. But for them it was only the beginning of the real story. All their life in this world and all their adventures in Narnia had only been the cover and the title page: now at last they were beginning Chapter One of the Great Story which no one on earth has read: which goes on forever: in which every chapter is better than the one before.[2]

Welcome to Chapter One

The literary genius of C. S. Lewis goes without saying, and nowhere is this more on display than at the conclusion to the Chronicles of Narnia. The paragraph quoted above has been most helpful in regard to bringing this study to its end. It is important that we conclude by highlighting not only how the book of Revelation ties together all loose ends in the biblical story, but also how it shows us a picture of a new life. It is no coincidence that Genesis (the book of the beginning) and Revelation (the book of the end) bear such remarkable language, and it is fitting to illustrate how the new creation concludes a perfect end to the Bible's overarching message.

Genesis introduces us to the original creation of the heavens and the earth (Gen 1:1); Revelation previews the coming new heavens and earth (Rev 21:1). Genesis outlines the creation of the heavenly bodies, the establishment of night, and the laying out of the sea (Rev 1:16, 5, 10); Revelation describes the absence of these things in what they symbolized (21:23; 22:5; 21:1).

Genesis introduces the great serpent and his cosmic deception (3:1); Revelation proclaims the defeat of the dragon (20:10). Genesis ushers in the curse of sin into the world along with the penalty of death (3:14–17, 19); Revelation announces the reversal of the curse and the death of death (22:3; 21:4). Genesis expels sinners from Eden (3:24); Revelation invites the saints into the gates of the new Jerusalem, where they will live as priest to their God and Christ for all eternity (22:14).

All of this proclaims that Revelation, while certainly being about the end of human history as we know it, is far more focused on the dawning of God's eternal reign over the cosmos as

---

2 Lewis, *The Last Battle*, 228.

He ushers in eternal life for His redeemed people. Revelation is the drama and narrative of how the new creation will come about through King Jesus.

We must not think of the eternal state as one in which we sit on clouds in heaven, playing our harps for all eternity. The arrival of the new creation is the beginning of an unending adventure story, one in which God's people live out a life far beyond what they could ever have imagined and far better than what they could have ever desired in this current age.

Revelation 21 and 22 is the promised consummation of the hope that Jesus inaugurated at His first coming. As the author Hebrews says, "Christ, having been offered once in order to bear the sins of many, will appear for the second time without reference to sin to those who eagerly await him for salvation" (9:28). Upon his second coming, Jesus administers the final judgment, where all redeemed believers receive an apocalyptic, symbol-laden picture of life beyond the eschaton. For Christians, the end is the new beginning.

I once saw a video that went viral on Facebook; it had a montage of people of all ages who were deaf and, due to the advances in technology, were caught on camera experiencing sound for the first time. It was so emotional that I had chills watching it. The looks on their faces as they heard what their loved ones sounded like for the first time said it all. One of the clips included a little child who, when the hearing device was turned on, was able to hear her mother singing to her, and the child started crying tears of joy.

What these people were experiencing, although new to them, wasn't foreign or far out; they were experiencing something human, something they were supposed to have experienced all along and never had the opportunity to experience till that moment—sound. Similarly, life in the new creation won't be like going off to some foreign land, in which the customs, language, or people make us feel like total outsiders who don't have a place there. It will instead feel like coming home after a long journey, and experiencing all of the nostalgia of what makes home, *home*. Our journey is about returning to a place we have never been. A place where the fullness of God's presence resides. Where we will be exposed to the unveiled, unfiltered, untamed glory of God!

Where Do We Go From Here?

Although we eagerly await our future hope, it is imperative that we also remind ourselves that salvation is also a present reality. However, like reverse engineering, our knowledge of the future provides invaluable insights into the present. We can only truly be present in the moment because we do not have to worry about what the future may bring our way. We know the future is bright, and this enables us to face the challenges of today. We can embrace the journey of this world and its trials because we know that dusk only lasts so long until the day breaks and the dawn of the new creation is here.

In 2 Cor 5:17, Paul reminds us that "if anyone is in Christ, he is a new creation; the old things have passed away; behold, new things have come." If we are truly followers of Christ, then these words are for us—we are a new creation! Paul's words do not mean that we have arrived at perfection now. What they do indicate, however, is that the resurrection glory and reigning power of Christ have been inaugurated in and through the life of Christians now.

While there is so much more to look forward to, this hope must not negate the will of God for His people living in the world today. We are a new creation, and Paul's assumption is that being in a relationship with Jesus should bring about a radical revolution in the life of a Christ follower.

Through the chapters in this book I have attempted to show how the whole story of the Bible is eschatological. Even Eden, that is sometimes portrayed as a perfect paradise, had further potential and thus served as a signpost for the new Eden. Instead of journeying through all of Scripture, we focused on the book of Revelation as the canonical capstone of the Bible to see how the apocalyptic letter's drama unveils the imminent new creation.

We examined two key scenes in Revelation; the throne room vision (4–5) and the vision of the new creation (21:1–22:5). The former vision acted as the interpretive key to understand the supreme message of the letter, where the Messiah's work on earth precedes His heavenly enthronement. Now, even before the consummation of new creation, he reigns alongside the Father in an inaugurated fashion. The "end-times" have been steadily in progress for 2,000 plus years now and we have a role in them. The latter vision gave us a glimpse (albeit, through apocalyptic symbolism) of what the new creation entails. Looking closely at the text of Rev 21–22:5, while also pulling from other important, supplemental texts, we filled in other key aspects of our great hope—centering these ideas on a fresh phrase: a resurrected cosmos.

It may help to reiterate the thesis found back in the introduction: *The climax of the story of redemption is a resurrected cosmos where the triune God and His redeemed, resurrected people will reign for eternity, unrivaled and infinitely satisfied with endless chapters of adventures to experience.*

The apex of our hope is a face-to-face relationship with the triune God (Rev 22:4). These wonderful truths are meant to grant us endurance as we hold on for our happy hope. We get to be the most optimistic people on the planet, knowing that the first Easter was a signpost of what God would do for all creation, especially those who trust him. More than only giving us a future hope, relishing eschatology gives us a fodder for a compelling story. We get to narrate the good story—by word and deed—acting as the seeds of new creation until it sprouts up and engulfs every spec of the animate and inanimate universe. Thus, our lives are given even greater meaning as we teach the world to trust the eschatological story of Scripture by being reconciled to God and living compelling lives in eager anticipation of the earth's King returning to set all things right and make all things new. Until then, may our hearts sing of our hope and our lives act with the glorious future in mind—bringing love, justice, and hope wherever we can even now.

Bibliography

Akin, Daniel L. *Exalting Jesus in Revelation*, Christ-Centered Exposition Series. Edited by David Platt, Daniel L. Akin, and Tony Merida. Nashville, TN: Holman Reference, 2016.

Arndt, William, Frederick W. Danker, Walter Bauer, and F. Wilbur Gingrich. *A Greek-English Lexicon of the New Testament and Other Early Christian Literature*. Chicago: University of Chicago Press, 2000.

Bauckham, Richard. *The Theology of the Book of Revelation*. Cambridge, United Kingdom: Cambridge University Press, 1993.

———. *Jesus and the God of Israel: God Crucified and Other Studies on the New Testament's Christology of Divine Identity*. Grand Rapids: Eerdmans, 2009.

Beale, G. K. *The Book of Revelation: A Commentary on the Greek Text*. NIGTC. Grand Rapids, MI; Carlisle, Cumbria: W. B. Eerdmans; Paternoster Press, 1999.

———. *The Temple and the Church's Mission: A Biblical Theology of the Dwelling Place of God*. NSBT 17. IVP, 2004.

———. *A New Testament Biblical Theology: The Unfolding of the Old Testament in the New*. Grand Rapids, MI: Baker Academic, 2011.

Beale, G. K. and D. A. Carson, *Commentary on the New Testament Use of the Old Testament*. Grand Rapids: Baker Academic, 2007.

Blomberg, Craig. *Matthew*. NAC 22. Nashville: Broadman & Holman Publishers, 1992.

Boesak, Allan A., *Comfort and Protest: Reflections on the Apocalypse of John of Patmos*. Philadelphia: Westminster, 1987.

Brand, Chad, Charles Draper, Archie England, Steve Bond, E. Ray Clendenen, Trent C. Butler, and Bill Latta, eds. *Holman Illustrated Bible Dictionary*. Nashville, TN: Holman Bible Publishers, 2003.

Brannan, Rick, Ken M. Penner, Israel Loken, Michael Aubrey, and Isaiah Hoogendyk, eds. *The Lexham English Septuagint*. Bellingham, WA: Lexham Press, 2012.

Bratcher, Robert G., and Howard Hatton. *A Handbook on the Revelation to John*. UBS Handbook Series. New York: United Bible Societies, 1993.

Brooks, Richard. *The Lamb Is All the Glory*. Welwyn Commentary Series. Darlington, England: Evangelical Press, 1986.

Burk, Denny, John G. Stackhouse Jr., Robin Parry, Jerry Walls, Preston Sprinkle, and Stanley N. Gundry. *Four Views on Hell: Second Edition*. Grand Rapids, MI: Zondervan, 2016.

Charlesworth, James H. *The Old Testament Pseudepigrapha*. Vol. 1. New York; London: Yale University Press, 1983.

Charnock, Stephen. *The Complete Works of Stephen Charnock.* Vol. 1–5. Edinburgh; London; Dublin: James Nichol; James Nisbet and Co.; W. Robertson; G. Herbert, 1864–1866.

Doriani, Daniel M. *NT252 Parables of Jesus.* Logos Mobile Education. Bellingham, WA: Lexham Press, 2014.

Edwards, Jonathan. *The Works of Jonathan Edwards.* Vol. 1. Banner of Truth Trust, 1974.

Elwell, Walter A., and Barry J. Beitzel. *Baker Encyclopedia of the Bible.* Grand Rapids, MI: Baker Book House, 1988.

Evans, Craig A., and Craig A. Bubeck, eds. *John's Gospel, Hebrews–Revelation.* First Edition. The Bible Knowledge Background Commentary. Colorado Springs, CO; Paris, ON; Eastbourne: David C Cook, 2005.

Fee, Gordon D. *Revelation.* New Covenant Commentary Series. Eugene, OR: Cascade Books, 2011.

Flavel, John. *The Whole Works of the Reverend John Flavel.* Vol. 1–6. London; Edinburgh; Dublin: W. Baynes and Son; Waugh and Innes; M. Keene, 1820.

Freedman, David Noel, Gary A. Herion, David F. Graf, John David Pleins, and Astrid B. Beck, eds. *The Anchor Yale Bible Dictionary.* New York: Doubleday, 1992.

———, Allen C. Myers, and Astrid B. Beck. *Eerdmans Dictionary of the Bible.* Grand Rapids, MI: W. B. Eerdmans, 2000.

Fyall, Bob. *Daniel: A Tale of Two Cities.* Focus on the Bible Commentary. Ross-shire, Great Britain: Christian Focus Publications, 1998.

Gardner, Paul. *Revelation: The Compassion and Protection of Christ.* Focus on the Bible Commentary. Ross-shire, Great Britian: Christian Focus Publications, 2002.

Goldingay, John. *Old Testament Theology: Israel's Gospel.* Vol. 1. Westmont: IVP Academic, 2003.

González, Catherine Gunsalus, and Justo L. González. *Revelation.* Edited by Patrick D. Miller and David L. Bartlett. Westminster Bible Companion. Louisville, KY: Westminster John Knox Press, 1997.

Goodwin, Thomas. *The Works of Thomas Goodwin.* Vol. 1. Edinburgh: James Nichol, 1861.

Heiser, Michael S. *The Unseen Realm: Recovering the Supernatural Worldview of the Bible.* Bellingham, WA: Lexham Press, 2015.

Hoekema, Anthony A. *The Bible and the Future.* Grand Rapids, MI; Cambridge, U.K.: William B. Eerdmans Publishing Company, 1994.

Larry W. Hurtado, *Lord Jesus Christ: Devotion to Jesus in Earliest Christianity.* Eerdmans, 2003.

Johnson Dennis E. *Triumph of the Lamb: A Commentary on Revelation.* Phillipsburg, NJ: P&R Publishing, 2001.

Kline, Meredith G. *God, Heaven and Har Magedon: A Covenantal Tale of Cosmos and Telos*. Eugene, OR: Wipf & Stock Publishers, 2006.

Kittel, Gerhard, and Gerhard Friedrich, eds. *Theological Dictionary of the New Testament*. Translated by Geoffrey W. Bromiley. 10 vols. Grand Rapids: Eerdmans, 1964–1976.

Macleod, Donald. *Jesus Is Lord: Christology Yesterday and Today*. Fearn, UK: Christian Focus Publications, 2000.

Mangum, Douglas, Derek R. Brown, Rachel Klippenstein, and Rebekah Hurst, eds. *Lexham Theological Wordbook*. Lexham Bible Reference Series. Bellingham, WA: Lexham Press, 2014.

Mathews, K. A. *Genesis 1-11:26*. NAC. Nashville: Broadman & Holman Publishers, 1996.

Matthews, Victor Harold, Mark W. Chavalas, and John H. Walton. *The IVP Bible Background Commentary: Old Testament*. Electronic ed. Downers Grove, IL: InterVarsity Press, 2000.

Middleton, J. Richard. *A New Heaven and a New Earth: Reclaiming Biblical Eschatology*. Grand Rapids, MI: Baker Academic, 2014.

Miller, Stephen R. *Daniel*. Vol. 18. The New American Commentary. Nashville: Broadman & Holman Publishers, 1994.

Milne, Bruce. *The Message of Heaven and Hell: Grace and Destiny*. The Bible Speaks Today. Downers Grove, IL: InterVarsity Press, 2002.

Morgan, Christopher W., and Robert A. Peterson, eds. *The Deity of Christ*. Theology in Community. Wheaton, IL: Crossway, 2011.

Morris, Leon. *The Apostolic Preaching of the Cross*. 3rd ed. Eerdmans, 1965.

———. *Revelation: An Introduction and Commentary*. Tyndale New Testament Commentaries 20. Downers Grove, IL: InterVarsity Press, 1987.

Mounce, Robert H. *The Book of Revelation*, revised edition. NICNT. Edited by F. F. Bruce and Gordon D. Fee. Grand Rapids: Eerdmans, 1977.

Ortlund, Raymond C., Jr., and R. Kent Hughes. *Isaiah: God Saves Sinners*. Preaching the Word. Wheaton, IL: Crossway Books, 2005.

Osborne, Grant R. *Revelation: Verse by Verse*. Osborne New Testament Commentaries. Bellingham, WA: Lexham Press, 2016.

Paul, Ian. *Revelation: An Introduction and Commentary*. Edited by Eckhard J. Schnabel. TNTC 20. London: IVP, 2018.

Peterson, David G. *The Acts of the Apostles*. The Pillar New Testament Commentary. Grand Rapids, MI; Nottingham, England: William B. Eerdmans Publishing Company, 2009.

Phillips, Richard D. *Reformed Expository Commentary: Revelation*. Philipsburg, New Jersey: P&R Publishing Company, 2017.

Resseguie, James L. *The Revelation of John: A Narrative Commentary.* Grand Rapids, MI: Baker Academic, 2009.

Richter, Sandra L. *Stewards of Eden: What Scripture Says about the Environment and Why It Matters.* Downers Grove, IL: IVP Academic, 2020.

Rutherford, Samuel., *Letters of Samuel Rutherford.* Edited by Andrew A. Bonar. Edinburgh and London: Oliphant Anderson and Ferrier, 1891.

Sanders, Fred. "Forever and Always the Son: Why We Treasure Eternal Generation." *Desiring God.* Last modified March 16, 2020. https://www.desiringgod.org/articles/forever-and-always-the-son.

Sibbes, Richard. *The Complete Works of Richard Sibbes.* Edited by Alexander Balloch Grosart. Vol. 4. Edinburgh; London; Dublin: James Nichol; James Nisbet and Co.; W. Robertson, 1863.

Silva, Moisés, ed. *New International Dictionary of New Testament Theology and Exegesis.* Grand Rapids, MI: Zondervan, 2014.

Smith, Gary V. *Isaiah 1–39.* Edited by E. Ray Clendenen. NAC. Nashville: B&H Publishing Group, 2007.

Spurgeon, C. H. *The Metropolitan Tabernacle Pulpit Sermons.* Vol. 14. London: Passmore & Alabaster, 1868.

———. *The Metropolitan Tabernacle Pulpit Sermons.* Vol. 27. London: Passmore & Alabaster, 1881.

———. *The Metropolitan Tabernacle Pulpit Sermons.* Vol. 49. London: Passmore & Alabaster, 1903.

———. *The Metropolitan Tabernacle Pulpit Sermons.* Vol. 51. London: Passmore & Alabaster, 1905.

———. *Morning and Evening: Daily Readings.* London: Passmore & Alabaster, 1896.

Studer, Basil. "Hypostatic Union." Pages 309–10 in *Encyclopedia of Ancient Christianity.* Edited by Angelo Di Berardino. Downers Grove: IVP Academic, 2014.

Thomas, Robert L. *Revelation 8–22: An Exegetical Commentary.* Chicago: Moody Press, 1995.

Trail, Ronald. *An Exegetical Summary of Revelation 1–11.* 2nd ed. Dallas, TX: SIL International, 2008.

———. *An Exegetical Summary of Revelation 12–22.* 2nd ed. Dallas, TX: SIL International, 2008.

Van der Toorn, Karel, Bob Becking, and Pieter Willem van der Horst. *Dictionary of Deities and Demons in the Bible.* Leiden; Boston; Köln; Grand Rapids, MI; Cambridge: Brill; Eerdmans, 1999.

Walaskay, Paul W. *Acts.* Edited by Patrick D. Miller and David L. Bartlett. Westminster Bible Companion. Louisville, KY: Westminster John Knox Press, 1998.

Wanamaker, Charles A. *The Epistle to the Thessalonians*. NIGTC. Eerdmans, 1990.

Wesley, John, and Charles Wesley. *The Poetical Works of John and Charles Wesley*. Edited by G. Osborn. Vol. 1. London: Wesleyan-Methodist Conference Office, 1868.

Wright, N. T. *Following Jesus: Biblical Reflections on Discipleship*. London: Society for Promoting Christian Knowledge, 1994.

———. *Paul for Everyone: Galatians and Thessalonians*. London: Society for Promoting Christian Knowledge, 2004.

———. *Surprised by Hope*. London: SPCK, 2007.

———. *Revelation for Everyone*. For Everyone Bible Study Guides. London; Louisville, KY: SPCK; Westminster John Knox, 2011.

———. *Surprised by Hope*. London: Society for Promoting Christian Knowledge, 2007.